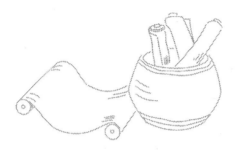

THE LOST SISTERHOOD

Julia Ingram

THE LOST SISTERHOOD

The Return of Mary Magdalene, the Mother Mary, and Other Holy Women

Julia Ingram

DreamSpeaker Creations 2004

This is a true story. The names of hypnosis subjects, unless otherwise noted, have been changed. Some scenes have been combined and edited for easier reading or better story presentation.

First printing: July 2004

Publication Data
    Ingram, Julia
    The Lost Sisterhood:
        The Return of Mary Magdalene, the Mother
        Mary, and Other Holy Women
    Inspiration, Spirituality, Women's Studies, New
        Consciousness
    pp. 184

    ISBN 1-893641-02-3
    1. Inspiration 2. Spirituality 3. New Consciousness

Cover design: Ken Elliott and G.W. Hardin
                Cover photo by Ken Elliott (ancient Coptic cloth fragment)
Book design: G.W. Hardin

Set in 11-point Palatino typeface
Printed in the United States of America

Published by DreamSpeaker Creations, Inc.
Fort Collins, Colorado • 2004

CONTENTS

THE LOST SISTERHOOD

INTRODUCTION

What if it were possible to read eyewitness reports revealing that the great prophet and healer Jesus Christ was influenced by the power of the women around him—Mary Magdalene, Mother Mary, and their contemporaries? How might our belief systems change if we learned that the healing talents of Jesus were preceded by those of his mother—and that his compassionate wisdom matured through his marriage to Mary Magdalene? How might our view of women's spiritual authority change if we learned that Mary Magdalene; her sister Martha; her sister-in-law Ruth; and other women were a critical part of Jesus' ministry?

In the Old Testament based religions that have shaped Western thought—Judaism, Islam, and Christianity—divine power has always been presented as utterly masculine. Only in recent years have both the scholarly research and the intuitive insights of women begun to balance the one-sided picture of Western religious history. Through the work of such researchers as Elaine Pagels, Marija Gimbutas, and Riane Eisler, we have gained glimpses of a long-suppressed, more feminine spiritual heritage. What we have lacked so far is a direct and intimate woman's-eye view into the very heart of sacred doctrine.

It was my disagreement—not only with patriarchal religions but also with the patriarchy within my profession of psychotherapy—that led me to transpersonal psychology. With the blending of psychology and Eastern spirituality, I was able to help my clients use the feminine quality of intuition, or *gnosis*, and to integrate mystical experiences into their everyday lives. About midway through my thirty-six years of practice, I introduced past-life regression therapy, with astonishingly positive results. Then, through a series of synchronistic events, I began seeing people who reported past lives during the time of Christ. My first book, *The Messengers*, co-written with G.W. Hardin, chronicles the story of one such client, Nick Bunick, who reported a past life of having been Paul, the Apostle. Among others who tapped into ancient times were dozens of women whose past-life stories and mystical experiences convinced me that the perspective of women was missing from most accounts of Jesus' mission and that Mary Magdalene's considerable role as a priestess in that spiritual revolution had been vastly underrated.

Drawing from the reports of fifteen women who came to me for past-life regressions, a powerful case is made that their underlying mission was much broader than traditional dogma suggests. The core purpose of Jesus' religious teachings was not such simple moralism as "Do unto others ... " but the metaphysical challenge to fully recognize the God and Goddess within everyone.

These historical visionaries revealed that the heart of the gospel was to restore balance between the male and the female by recognizing and honoring the equality of masculine and feminine traits within oneself, as well as the equality of the sexes in the outside world. As a young girl, Mother Mary studied at the Mount Carmel Monastery, and together she and Jesus sought to overcome the fundamentalism of the male-dominated Hebrew religion, returning the Mother God to her place alongside the Father. They taught that the Kingdom of God was within, rather than a place in the hereafter, and that through androgyny—"When you make the two one ... and when you make the inner as the outer"—an individual could experience the reality of heaven on earth.

The women in Jesus' life were not just servants or temptresses but his teachers, friends, lovers, and co-creators. They taught him in his youth, participated in healings, formed a community of support around him based on their own intuitive insights, and continued teaching the Gospel after his death. This Sisterhood of compassion was a critical component of Jesus's powerful message, yet until now it has not been recognized or validated.

The reports of these women change the common picture of the religious past in ways that reverberate powerfully in the present, and they are now being validated by recent translations and interpretations of the Nag Hammadi Library. Current research, scholarship, and my own observations support what my subjects reported under hypnosis.

The stories of *The Lost Sisterhood* come from women who have reported lives as Myrium (or Mary, Jesus' mother), Ruth (Jesus' younger sister), Martha (sister of Lazarus and Mary Magdalene), Mary Magdalene, and other holy women. Through past-life hypnotic sessions, these and other clients testify that women were an integral part of Jesus' ministry and personal life. They report that his mother, Mary, was a powerful teacher herself, a mystic who studied in Asia along with Jesus and was said to have had direct knowledge of spiritual matters. The women recount how Mary Magdalene tapped directly into the Divine Source and led an underground of women mystics. Most dramatically, however, they witness Jesus and Mary Magdalene as husband and wife, insisting that the union was necessary for Jesus to come fully into his spiritual power.

In further sessions, these women also bitterly reported that soon after Jesus' death, the men began to push them aside. One woman, Sarah of Arimathea, claims she wrote extensively during her apostleship but that her writings exist nowhere in Christian literature today. Many of my clients asserted that when women were pushed out of the inner circle, key aspects of the mission were lost. Consequently, their goals of peace and balance—to be at one with the God/Goddess within and to love one another accordingly—have yet to be attained.

Whether one regards these women's reports as real or imagined, their provocative messages are undeniable: Women are tired of being left out of the history of spiritual evolution. We are tired of being portrayed only as the silent handmaidens of male prophets, tired of being subject to religious laws without participating in their creation, and tired of being the victims of religious wars. *The Lost Sisterhood* presents a revisioning of our religious past that will help to shape our spiritual future.

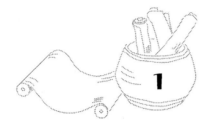

1

EXCOMMUNICATION

Portland, Oregon, 1976

I sobbed as I read the registered letter I'd just received. It was a notice of my excommunication from the Mormon Church.

Religion can be a dominant force in families. It was in mine. And when, in the mid-1970s, I decided I could no longer accept the dogma of the patriarchal religion of my parents, I might as well have cut out my heart. I know my request to be excommunicated sent a shock wave through my family. The only way to get my name off the records and to stop the monthly visits of well-meaning but unwanted visitors from the Church was to request excommunication—a violent term for a difficult process. There was no way to slip quietly away from this Church, either. The names of those who have "fallen away" are read from the pulpit during a church service.

The decision to be true to my own spiritual longing and to walk my own path was painful. While it shouldn't be so in a country where religious freedom is a right, and while leaving the

Mormon religion wasn't a crime, for years after my excommunication I felt guilty—and angry. What gave the men in my family the authority to be God's representatives? And why had the women bought into such a belief?

During the remainder of the 1970s and early 1980s, I longed for a spiritual community, but I could not abide the subservience of women in most of the religions I investigated. I needed to know why women have had little part in shaping and interpreting spiritual matters. My heart and my mind told me there was something very wrong with the fundamental dogmas of patriarchal religions.

When the heart asks questions of Spirit, answers often come in the form of experiences. Mine began in 1980 when I traveled in Japan, Hong Kong, Singapore, and Indonesia. These are all places populated by people for whom reincarnation and past lives are a fact of life. While at that time I had no personal experiences to support such a belief myself, I rather hoped it was true. It made no sense that we would have only one lifetime.

A few years later I attended a personal growth workshop offered by a company called Context Trainings, in which participants were assisted to confront all of the ways in which we sabotaged our own success and happiness. During closed-eye exercises, I became increasingly frustrated with my inability to visualize. My fellow trainees reported colorful visions, powerful messages, delightful messengers—while I was seeing exactly nothing. A friend recommended a hypnotist whom she thought could help me learn to visualize. What did I have to lose?

When I called for an appointment, the receptionist asked if I wanted to stop smoking, lose weight, or have a past-life regression. Since I didn't smoke and weight wasn't an issue, that left regression. *Kill two birds with one stone,* I thought. I'd wondered about past lives since my Asia trip. Maybe with this hypnotist I'd be able to open up my inner vision far enough to see into the distant past.

I went to the appointment excited, but doubtful. While I used hypnosis in my own counseling practice, I didn't think I would be a good subject myself. Adam greeted me with a warm handshake; his voice was the kind of rich baritone that announcers on classical radio stations have. He was a big man with a shock of silver-white hair and a full beard—*one part guru, one part Santa Claus,* I thought. He led me into a dimly lit office, simply furnished with two large recliners and a table full of recording equipment, and fitted me with headphones. This seemed strange at first but, as I leaned back into the recliner, I heard the pleasant strains of Kitaro's *Silk Road,* and then Santa Claus began to speak.

To my great surprise, I went into a deep hypnotic trance and, with Adam's prodding, began to report what I saw in my mind's eye. I was a small boy, about ten years old, looking down at my mother's grave. When Adam asked what had happened to my mother, I suddenly saw the inside of our dark one-room house. While I stood by watching helplessly from a corner, my father, red-faced and raging, was beating my mother for not making the fire to his liking. My small, young mother was crouched in another corner, trying to ward off his blows with her thin hands. She screamed and pleaded, but the beating continued—until she was dead. I had been paralyzed with shock and fear the whole time.

In response to Adam's questions about when and where this took place, I answered without hesitation: "1081 BC., somewhere in ... now it's called Jordan. I see pink sand. Our very small house is of bricks made from this sand." As the regression continued, I reported many details.

While I was seeing all of these images, my logical present-life mind was at the same time wondering, *Where is all this coming from?* Fortunately, Adam quickly pulled me back into the experience by asking me to focus on the last few years in that lifetime. I told him of battles I was forced to fight in order to protect our town, of my term as governor, and finally of my assassination by political enemies.

Most astonishing of all, I remembered rising up out of my body and observing my funeral. Afterwards I floated into a large Greek- or Roman-style building where hundreds of scrolls, each about three feet high, stood upright, lining the walls of the circular room. I understood that this library represented the history of my soul—past, present, and future. In that moment, I also understood the concept of time/no time. I saw the vastness of myself and how much experience I, as soul, have had and will have. I understood that I have all the time that I need to achieve my soul's desires.

For three days following this experience I felt disoriented. Thrilled, expanded, I was totally without fear. I was not the same woman I had been three days before. My spiritual eyes had been opened, and I finally understood why certain themes kept running through my life: a compulsive desire to protect the weak, terrible fear whenever I heard the voice of an angry person, a willingness and ability to assume leadership, and others.

All in one two-hour regression session, I thought. This was a powerful tool! Adam wasn't even a formally trained therapist. *Think what I, as a therapist, could do with a tool like this.*

I called Adam and arranged to train with him so I could guide others into past lives. Hungrily, I devoured books by Dick Sutphen, Helen Wambaugh, Ruth Montgomery, and others, practicing on anyone who was willing to give this technique a try. After becoming proficient in this very effective new technique, I joined the Association of Past-Life Research and Therapies.

It was not long afterwards that a series of remarkable women and men found their way to my office, taking me even deeper into healing and knowledge through past-life regression—and turning what I had learned as a child about Christianity on its head.

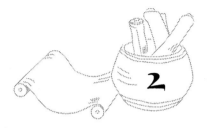

RUTH AND THE BLUE LADY

When Carol called for an appointment, she said a psychic had told her that the root of her medical problems, as well as their cure, lay in a previous life and that past-life regression work would be of great benefit to her. She had been diagnosed with the serious and sometimes fatal autoimmune disease lupus. Carol had never been hypnotized before and wasn't at all sure she could be, but she turned out to be an excellent hypnosis subject. In fact, Carol was one who *relived* past lives more than she *reported* them.

During one session, she recalled a life in which she had died while pregnant. Two days later, she called and reported symptoms of pregnancy—an impossibility, she said, in her current incarnation. Another time, after reporting a past life as a pirate, she complained of a craving for whisky and a compulsion for cursing! From working with Carol, I learned that I had to be very careful always to instruct the client's present body not to take on any physical characteristics of recalled past lifetimes.

During Carol's first session, the story that appeared in her mind's eye seemed to point to a possible reason she had lupus in this lifetime. She reported a poignant story of her life as Elizabeth, a young Englishwoman whose father took her to live in the Spice Islands (modern Grenada) in the 1800s. There, she fell in love with a seaman. The night before he shipped out, they stood on the beach at sunset and pledged their love, planning to marry when he returned. But he did not return. Several months after their engagement, she learned that his ship had been attacked and had sunk with no survivors. She said that when she lost her great love she lost all will to live. Within a short time she died, with her last thought being, *I cannot live without him.*

How fascinating, I thought. *Can chronic illness be the result of decisions made or events lived in previous lifetimes?*

I asked, "Carol, do you have the will to live a full life at this time?" She replied, "Yes, I do. I'm not like Elizabeth. I want to live, and I want to be healthy so I can really enjoy my work, my friends, and playing with my grandchildren."

I coached her to work with that aspect of herself that is Elizabeth—to mourn the loss of her lover but to see that she could make a choice to live a full life without him. Carol understood and declared, "I stand on my own. My heart is still open to love, but I claim my own life force. This lupus no longer has a place in my life."

About six months into our work together, we had made great headway in clearing the lupus. That day, Carol regressed to a past life which astounded me. As she moved into the experience, she appeared to become younger. She had a very shy look on her face.

"Hello," I said gently. "What is your name?"

"I'm Ruth." Her voice was high-pitched and her inflection childlike.

"Hello, Ruth. How old are you?"

"I'm six. Are you an angel?"

"No, dear. I'm just a lady. But I am talking to you from far away."

"Oh. You are blue. My angel says I can call you the Blue Lady."

"There's an angel with you today?"

"There are always angels with me."

"And this one said to call me the Blue Lady?"

"Uh huh. She says you are nice. She's the Pink Angel."

I told Ruth I was happy her angel was with us. She blushed and beamed. She seemed especially sweet. I asked her where she lived and with whom she was living. She said she lived in Palestine with her mother, father, and brothers. I asked her to move into her high self and give me the approximate year of this memory, and she replied that it was two thousand years ago.

"Tell me about your mother," I said.

"Oh. She is so beautiful. She loves to sing and dance. She is very happy. But sometimes she is sad."

"Why is she sometimes sad?"

"Because Jeshua has to go away to study."

"Jeshua?"

"Yes, my big brother is Jeshua."[1]

OK, Julia, I said to myself, *you had no trouble accepting Carol's lifetime as the tragic heroine of the Spice Islands, the bawdy pirate, the pregnant pioneer who died traveling west. But now, just as matter-of-factly as in all her other stories, she is reporting being the little sister of Jesus?* My first thought was, *How is she going to handle this?* My second thought was, *How am I?* Most of my regression clients had recalled impactful lifetimes, but they were lives as ordinary people. Still, well-known people must reincarnate, just as we ordinary ones do. *Anyway,* I told myself, *regression work isn't fact-finding.*

"What are you doing today, Ruth?"

"Jeshua is teaching me how to mend my puppy's broken leg."

"What does he teach you?"

"To see in my mind that the bone is already better. We just hold my puppy and touch the leg, and it is better."

"What else are you learning?"

"How to fly. Mother and Jeshua are teaching me how to fly. But I have to stay in my room. I'm too little to fly out of the house

---

1. Jeshua is the Aramaic version of the Master's name, while Jesus is the Greek version. Most of my clients who report lifetimes during that era use Jeshua because that was the name by which they knew him.

yet. I want to go with him. He says when I'm a little older we will fly someplace interesting together."

I thought it likely she was talking about astral travel, the ability some people have when their consciousness (or astral body) can leave the physical body and go other places.

At the close of this session, Carol and I talked a bit. She said she was excited to be so in tune with that ancient part of her that was learning how to heal. She knew she would be using these recalled abilities to help others in the near future. I asked her what she thought about the Pink Angel and Ruth calling me the Blue Lady. She said, "What I'm hearing is that these colors are about vibration. The Pink Angel's main vibration is sweet love; she surrounds little Ruth with this love. They tell me that when you are working with people, your principal vibration is of compassion, and that is a blue color."

Cool, I thought. *I know that when I work with people my heart is open and my attention is totally focused on being of service.* It was fascinating to think that there are colors associated with intention. It made sense, though, because everything, even thought, is vibration. I thanked Carol for the information, and we scheduled another appointment for two weeks later.

In this next session, Carol again recalled her little Ruth lifetime.

"Where do we find you today?"

"It is hot and bright. I go into the house to get a drink. Father starts tickling me and Mother.

Mother is laughing. After I get my drink, I go out and play with my doll. We are having a party. Somebody is calling me. My Pink Angel. She wants me to come and see something. We are going to the shed. Our dog is having puppies. The angel wants me to see the mother giving birth. She has me run my hand on the dog's spine. It eases her. She stops whining. There is time in between the puppies, so I am running my hands down the stomach area; it eases her tension. It is fun. She is having the last puppy ... she has five. I run my hands down the spine and to the stomach area and stuff comes out. The Pink Angel says I'm helping my dog. Now I'm putting fresh straw down for her, and she is lying down with puppies all cuddling next to her.

"The Pink Angel wants me to talk about what I did. I ran my energy through the dog to ease the pain. My energy came through as purple, sometimes changing to gold. I saw it and changed it by seeing it. It doesn't go out of my hands until I can see it. If I see it, then I know it is the right color. That is what Mother has taught me. I go to tell Mother that the puppies are all right, and she tells me I did really well."

"Thank you, Ruth. Please move to another significant event now."

"The Pink Angel wants me to tell you we are going to go on a journey. I'll be leaving soon. We are going to Mother's community [Mount Carmel] to visit. We are leaving in three days, and it will take us three or four days to get there. My brother is not here; he is at the community already, studying. Mother is excited. She is saying my brother has learned something that is very important."

"Please move forward to your arrival."

"I am taking a nap because I am tired. When I wake up, we have all the family around. Mother's cousin Rebecca—she's really nice, I like her. Rebecca's brother, Rebecca's children, Timothy and Joseph. They are funny. They are just funny, ten and twelve years old. I'm too little for them to play with me. My brother plays with me, takes me on his shoulders, carrying me around. We are going to his teacher's room now. I like riding on his shoulders [laughing]. His teacher is a funny little man: short, round, spindly legs like toothpicks, funny hair that sticks out all over his head.

"We are sitting on the floor, and Jeshua wants to show me what he has learned. He puts a small coin in the palm of his left hand, puts his right hand next to his left, and the coin moves across his left hand to his right. It stays on his hand. He is all excited that he got to do this. Jeshua wanted to be able to do this before he turned eighteen [a little more than a year away]. The coin moved with his mind. There will be times that things will be moved through the energy of the hands, but now he's doing it just with his mind. This is the first step. His teacher wants him to go far away to practice. This is his graduation day after four years of study. The teacher's name starts with *s*. Sabbusis? I don't understand this language; it is hard to translate. We are going to go back home. Jeshua will be going to the land that has lots of mountains."

Carol told me later that she could see that the teacher was from Tibet and that Jeshua had been invited to go there for further study.

"Please move to another significant event."

"I'm five. Mother teaches me every day. It's important to practice every day. I practice 'not seeing.' I need to start not seeing the walls, furniture, other things. I need to see beyond them because they are not solid. Mother has me look at a bowl, and then I need to tell her what I see in between that is not there. Sometimes I can see things, sometimes not. I tell her when I can see things. She instructs me how to look beyond the bowl. I stare at the bowl but look beyond it; I start to see through the bowl. Sometimes she will put different colored water in the bowl, and I will tell her what the water looks like and what it doesn't look like. She explains about energy. The bowl isn't solid; nothing is. She is teaching me to see beyond the solid. There are times when I get frustrated, but she tells me I am doing well."

As this session came to a close, Carol and I discussed what she had reported. I observed that it was remarkable the way she was using visualization to teach herself, in effect, how to work with energy and to heal herself of lupus. She agreed but added, "I am also convinced that I *was* Ruth and that Jesus was my older brother. This material is not just symbolic. It's real. There is a reason I'm remembering this today."

I asked, "What are you making of this? You said Mary was part of the Mount Carmel community and that she was a teacher, too. And you, as Ruth, were being instructed just as Jeshua was— to comfort and heal. The Bible doesn't mention this at all or that Jeshua had a little sister."

Carol frowned. "The Bible leaves out half the story. The women were a very significant part of Jeshua's mission. Mary was his first teacher. I can feel how powerful she was and how bright Ruth was as well. Not only have the women been left out of the story, but a lot of the messages Jeshua came to teach have been distorted."

"Like what?"

"Like the concept of sin. My brother didn't teach about sin. He taught love and compassion. After Jeshua died, another brother, James, took on a leadership role, but he didn't listen to Mother. He started manipulating people with fear. They got it wrong!"

"Whew. That is quite a revelation, Carol. I would love to learn more about what you seem to be remembering."

"You will," she laughed. "They [her spirit guides, whom she began calling the Teachers] are telling me that there is much more to come."

During her next session, the Teachers announced, "We have a message for you, Julia." Since the Teachers had proved themselves to be loving in the ways they had helped Carol, I felt open to receiving a message from them.

Carol's Teachers spoke, using her voice. "You have a contract,[2] dear sister, with your soul group, to be a record keeper and to recover lost information from after Jeshua's death. You will meet many women and men who shall provide pieces of the story of how the Christian movement was thrown out of balance when it eliminated the Mother God from its theology and the effects this disharmony has had on civilization. Other assignments will be revealed at a later time. We will help you to learn to listen to your own wise self and to other spirit guides, who will from time to time present themselves as assistants."

I wasn't sure what to make of this, but I was intrigued. I thanked Carol and the Teachers warmly. These were the issues with which I had been grappling, myself, for at least a decade. The Jesus of whom I instinctively knew and loved could not have endorsed the dogma of some Christian religions of today.

---

2. For information on this subject, read Caroline Myss, *Sacred Contracts: Awakening Your Divine Potential* (New York, 2002).

THE MYSTERY OF MOUNT CARMEL

*L*ittle Ruth said that her mother, Myrium, was part of the Mount Carmel community and that she taught there. Ruth was being instructed—just as Jeshua was—to comfort and to heal. Carol's words haunted me: "The Bible leaves out half the story. The women were a very significant part of Jeshua's mission. Not only have the women been left out of the story, but a lot of the messages Jeshua came to teach have been distorted."

I was curious, however, about the contradiction between what I'd been hearing from Ruth and those in the modern Gnostic movement—that Jeshua sprang from an enlightened Essene community in which women were active and honored—and what I had surmised from reading the New Testament and from what history suggested.

The Essenes were a minor and unusual sect of Judaism. The Pharisees and Sadducees constituted the two major branches. Translations of Essene scriptures from the Dead Sea scrolls and descriptions of life at the Qumran monastery written by historians from that time suggest that the Essenes were extremely strict—and extremely patriarchal. The celibate life of the monastery (which was for men only) was much more highly regarded than were marriage and family life in the outlying communities. The Jewish historian Josephus, himself a member of the monastery, wrote of women:

> They [Qumran Essenes] do not, indeed on principle, condemn wedlock—the propagation thereby of the race, but they wish to protect themselves against women's wantonness, being persuaded that none of the sex keeps her plighted troth to one man.[3]

Philo, the Alexandrian scholar, revealed even greater misogyny among the Essenes:

> For no Essene takes a wife, because a wife is a selfish creature, excessively jealous and an adept at beguiling the morals of her husband and seducing him by her continued impostures. For by the fawning talk which she practices and the other ways in which she plays her part like an actress on the stage, she first ensnares the sight and hearing, and then, when these victims have, as it were, been duped, she cajoles the sovereign mind.[4]

I hoped to have the opportunity to learn more about the Essenes through spiritual eyes and, as the Teachers had predicted, I did.

When I met Deborah at a Noetic Science conference, she seemed somehow very familiar, although we had never met before. A tall, lanky woman in her sixties from the Southwest, she immediately impressed me as strong, intelligent, and independent. A retired psychotherapist and college professor, she was also a past-life regressionist with many years of experience in this field. She said she'd been a teacher for many lifetimes and was glad to be retired from all of them. She entertained me with stories of her life in the desert with three mongrel dogs, chickens, and goats.

As we shared our experiences over dinner, I sensed that she had worked with compassion and great skill with people who had had paranormal experiences. Finally, we got around to our own

---

3. Edmund Wilson, *The Scrolls from the Dead Sea* (New York: Oxford University Press, 1956), p. 28.
4. Ibid, p. 29.

past lives, and Deborah told me that she was a reincarnated Essene. I asked her what she understood about these puzzling Essenes.

"According to my own spiritual memory banks," she said slowly, seeming to look far away from the present in her mind's eye, "Myrium—the Aramaic version of her name, Mary being the Greek—the mother of Jeshua, was born into an Essene community which was quite different from most of the others scattered over the hills and deserts of Judea, Samaria, and Galilee. These particular Essenes abhorred politics. They preferred to hide out rather than be involved in the continuous battles the other Jews had with the Syrians. As to other ways in which they were different, more liberal—well, I think I had something to do with that in the past life I spoke of."

Curious, I offered to regress Deborah, and she readily agreed. She suggested we meet in her room after the afternoon sessions were over. Putting her in the light hypnotic trance I generally use for this work, we began.

"Just relax, and as the picture develops, tell me where you find yourself today," I prompted.

"I live near Sepphoris [between Nazareth and Magdala]."

"And what is your name? What are you called by your family?"

"My name is Suddee."

"Please reach into your spirit mind and tell me what year it is, from present-day reckoning."

"It is about 165 B.C."

Extended family groups of Jews had sought refuge in nearby hills or desert regions around Palestine. History tells us that this was around the time that a family of guerrilla warriors, the Maccabees, defeated the Syrians against overwhelming odds. These were obviously difficult times for Jews. While she was still accessing information from her spirit mind, I asked her to tell me how she knew about the community to which Myrium, the mother of Jeshua, would belong.

"I was shown in a vision that I would found a monastery where the mother of the Christ would come to study one day. I was further shown that students from this monastery would receive training to prepare to provide support for her son."

"Please, go back in that lifetime to when you were younger, so we can learn more about what led up to this."

She took a deep breath and rotated her head in a circular fashion. A few seconds passed, and she answered.

"I am thirteen years old and the daughter of Joseph and Abdorah."

"Thank you, Suddee. Is there something special about turning thirteen in your community?"

"Yes [frowning]; for the boys, but not for girls. There is nothing for us."

"You sound unhappy about that," I said.

"It isn't fair. The boys get to study all day long until they pass the tests, and then they are honored in a big ceremony. I even have to sit way in the back."

"And you don't think it is fair." Her expression was one of a pouty teenager. Her lower lip covered the upper.

"For two years I have been asking my father and my brother what is in the scrolls and books they read. They won't tell me. I can read. My mother has taught me to read, but they won't let me read the holy books. My father said it is forbidden for me to even touch them."

"He says it is forbidden?"

"He says I shame him for even asking."

"Do you feel ashamed?"

"I feel mad! Is God only for boys? It isn't right." She looked as angry as she sounded. She heaved a big sigh. "I talk to my mother about it."

"How does that go?"

"Well [an even deeper sigh of resignation, now looking more sad than angry], she doesn't get upset like my father. She says she understands my being curious. She even agrees it isn't fair, but she says it's a long, long tradition that the men study the Scriptures and take care of the temples and the holy books, and that the women support them in their studies. She says that tradition is what holds the community together, especially because we Jews have to stick together. We have so many enemies."

"What do you think of her answer?"

"She said [that] to allow me to study the holy books would create problems. She told me to keep my anger to myself. [Speaking softly] I will obey my mother and not anger my father."

"Go on. What happens next?"

"I have a brother two years older than me. His name is Samuel. We go for walks along the streams in the canyons. He is telling me about what he's studying. He thinks I'm smart, and he likes to teach me what he is being taught. He even sneaked a book for me to read myself. I must be very careful. Father will be enraged at both of us if he finds out."

"It looks like you found a way to study in spite of it being forbidden."

"It seems to me that God speaks to girls as well as boys."

"What is the book Samuel gave you?"

"Deborah [her current incarnation] calls it the *Book of Exodus*. It is about our people when they were imprisoned in Egypt and how God helped them to leave."

"What is your favorite part?"

She brightened up. "I'm reading about Miriam, the sister of Moses. This is how I know women should serve God, too. She did. She led the women through the sea. They followed her. She stood up to Moses, too, when she didn't agree with him. He listened to her. He isn't like our rabbi, or my father."

"What would happen if you stood up to your rabbi?"

She gasped, the color draining from her face. "I could be killed!"

"Oh my. No wonder your mother cautioned you to keep your feelings to yourself."

"Well [shrugging her shoulders], I really got in trouble anyway. At dinner I asked father to tell me about Mother God. He stood up and told me that was blasphemy. He asked if I'd been speaking with some of the pagan girls from a neighboring village, to give me such thoughts. I said no. He struck me across the face." She put her hands to her face and wept. "I ran out of the house."

How, I wondered, *was this bright and courageous young woman going to manage in this oppressive community banded so rigidly together during a time of great danger, of possible extermination?* I asked her to move forward to age sixteen.

"I do the marketing for the family now. I have a strong back and long legs and can make the walk into Sepphoris in three hours. Today, I'm to buy cloth and oil and some spices. I love to bargain for the spices and to look at the beautiful fabrics, which come from the East."

"Please recall a significant day at the marketplace."

"Well, there are two women also buying spices, and we begin to talk. They are sisters. They weren't born here; they are from the North. They are Greek, but they live here now. They invite me to take refreshments."

"What do you talk about over refreshments?"

"Oh, about our families and friends. They tell me they have tutors and not only read and write, but also speak several languages and study mathematics, astronomy, and music."

"These must be the pagans your father warned you about."

"They are wonderful. They laugh and are so happy. The sisters love to dance like me. But in their family, girls also study. I ache for that."

"Do you see them again?"

"Oh, yes. I volunteer for all the shopping trips and meet them about once a month. I have met their parents and their astronomy tutor. He showed me charts and maps and told me the names of the big stars." Suddenly, Suddee stopped talking. She dropped her hands into her lap and bit her lip. I asked if something were troubling her.

"They lend me books, which I hide in the bottom of the baskets. I'm very careful with them."

"Suddee, are you able to keep all this to yourself?"

"Well, see, that's the trouble. I start to tell some other girls about what I'm learning. I start to read to some of them—at first just two. But eventually, twenty-two girls are coming."

"Oh my. Twenty-two girls?"

"Yes, and the secret gets out. Several parents discover what I'm doing. They go to my father, and he is furious and says I've shamed him. Then he finds out I have been teaching about the female God!"

"You are in serious trouble."

"I am beaten and forbidden to talk at all to the other girls in the village."

Suddee's precious books were not discovered, however. She managed to return them to her Greek friends but had to tell them she would not be able to see them again. They offered her refuge, which she considered, but she then decided to return home out of loyalty to her mother. We moved forward in time.

"I'm nineteen, and I'm unmarriageable. My mother and aunts tell me no man will have me because I do not know how to obey. I live with my parents."

"You sound unhappy."

"My only comfort is visiting my brother and playing with his babies."

"Please move forward to the next significant event."

"I'm walking along a stream in the canyon [frowning]. I'm being followed. Oh, it's three of the girls I'd been teaching. They tell me how much they miss the teachings ... that they wish to continue learning about God. I can't believe this, but they say their fathers are old-fashioned and beg me to teach them again. They say they are old enough to keep the meetings a secret."

"What do you decide?"

"I have missed the conversations, the stretching of my mind, and I give in. I say yes."

"Go on. What happens next?"

"It's a few days later. I'm out walking. It is midday and the sun is hot. I stop to rest inside the mouth of a small, cool cave." She spoke in a soft, sleepy voice. "I begin to doze. [Breathing in sharply] I'm suddenly aware of a presence. I turn and see a bright shimmering light. Blues, purples, flecks of silver begin to form themselves into the shape of a being—a beautiful woman." She had a look of wonder on her face. "She speaks: 'Fair sister, divine consort of God. It is time for you to become fully awake. You have a part to play in the awakening of the human race. Thousands of years ago, humans were put to sleep. It is now time for you to awaken into who you fully are. Mother God has been in the background. It was part of the plan. You have been experiencing what life becomes when one side of the human equation dominates. It is out of balance at this time. Now, Mother God is planning an awakening, and you are one of her handmaidens.'"

She appeared to be in a very deep trance, mesmerized. "This being reaches out her shimmering finger and touches my mind. [Gasping] I am knocked off my feet." Her voice became strong. "In a blinding flash, I see that I am to teach what I am being taught and that more will be revealed to me in the months to come." She was breathless and quickly became sad. "I am shown that I will be driven from the village by the rabbi and that I will go to Mount Carmel and found a school for women. [Smiling] I am shown that my friends, the Greek women, will give me money for the construction of buildings and the purchase of books." She began to weep. The look on her face reminded me of a Renaissance painting—delicate and full of light.

"I ... I'm shown that in several decades the mother of the long-awaited Messiah will study in this school and that by then it will be accepted and common for girls to study right alongside the boys in our community." She was silent for several seconds, then began to weep, her voice almost a whisper. "I am shown that the Anointed One will be a student in the monastery when he is a young man." Tears ran down my cheeks now, too. I realized I was rooting for Suddee and moved by her extraordinary experience.

Suddee slept for several hours after this vision took place. When she awoke, it was almost dark. She hurried back to her family's house, and all night long she pondered what had happened. She spent the next day in prayer, asking for the strength to carry out the luminous being's assignment.

"In my heart, I know I was born to do this. Miriam, the sister of Moses, is my ancestor, after all."

"I'm eager to hear what happens next, Suddee."

"Three days later, I gather my little group of women together and tell them what happened, and what I was shown would come to pass." She took a deep breath and set her jaw. "It's now two weeks later, and the rabbi has found out that I'm meeting with the girls. He roars at me, 'In spite of my warning and in defiance of your father and myself?' I feel calm. The being told me this would happen. The rabbi says, 'You must leave here and never return. If you ever set foot in the village again, you will be condemned to death. There are now two charges of blasphemy against you, Daughter. You are lucky I am compassionate, or you would already be dead!'"

Suddee gathered up her meager belongings—a few clothes, a necklace given to her by her grandmother, her precious books— and prepared to leave. Her mother was heartbroken, and her brother was angry—at Suddee, at himself for giving her that first book, and most of all at the situation. Samuel, his family, and Suddee's mother walked with her to the road leading to Sepphoris. They wept as they told her farewell, believing they would never see her again. Suddee never did see her family again, nor did she ever return to her village.

"A half day's walk brings me to the home of the Greek sisters, a trip I made so happily in past years. I didn't know if they would take me in."

"And did they?"

"They said they had been expecting me. I was so thrilled. I told them everything I had experienced with the beautiful being. They didn't question it. In fact, one said, 'Dear sister, you have been divinely called, and we will play our part to help you. In fact, we wish to be students.' 'But you are Greeks,' I said. The other sister said, 'Your visions are neither Greek nor Hebrew, nor of any old religion. You are preparing the way for the One to be understood. We will be honored to be a part of this monastery, this school.'"

"Please move several years into the future now. *Were* you able to create this monastery on Mount Carmel?"

"Oh, yes. It was only for women; they were bright and eager pupils. We were given much instruction from the angelic realm.

My friends' mother taught there from time to time, also. We taught not only the mysteries of ancient Greece and Egypt, but also of the legacy of the women from the Hebrew Scriptures. In addition, we were given scrolls that had been hidden for many centuries which told of our beginnings as radiant light, translated into human bodies. We were then in constant communion with our Divine Mother God."

The three village girls who had persuaded Suddee to resume their classes moved to the monastery. Many others followed. "Does any pupil stand out in your memory?" I asked.

She immediately answered, "Elizabeth. I remember ... I was in my fifties. She was invited to study in Tibet by monks who had visited our monastery earlier. Although she had a woman's body, she looked more like a boy. She was strong and brave, able to pass as male and therefore travel alone, which a female could not do. She dressed in boys' clothing and went by boat around to southern India. From there, she walked and sometimes rode a horse to the monastery in Tibet. She learned the language and became a monk there. She wrote to me often. She taught some of the monks our language and our traditions. She was a bridge between our monastery and theirs. She never returned to Mount Carmel, although some of her students did come here later."

"Thank you for telling me about Elizabeth. Like you, she was very brave. Suddee, I would appreciate hearing how what you taught was different from other schools."

"I did away with many of the old rules and rituals of my fathers, because the purpose behind them had been forgotten and so distorted that they now were meaningless. The villagers seemed to be taking their slow time about reconsidering whether the old ways suited us in our modern times. We taught no meaningless ritual in my school."

"No meaningless ritual. Is there meaningful ritual?"

"I taught practices. A practice brings one closer to Divine Light."

"Will you give an example?"

"Yes. Singing, or toning certain notes of the scale. Just walking alone near a stream, or baking bread. These bring one closer to Divine Mother/Father God."

By the following generation, Suddee's home village could not withhold education from girls. Every woman demanded it. The old rabbi died and, with him, went many of the old ways.

After I brought Deborah out of the hypnotic trance, she told me that Suddee died in her late seventies, very close to what would now be called 100 B.C. From her spirit mind she was able to see that two of La-Bet's (as her pupil Elizabeth was called in Tibet) students would go to Mount Carmel. These two monks would teach the Essenes how to meditate in their method. They would also teach about chanting, astral travel, and how to work with energy. In addition, she foresaw that a second generation of monks would be present during the preparation for the conception of Jeshua and would remain to assist in keeping Myrium's energy high during her pregnancy. Deborah said that Myrium would learn some of the Tibetan language from these monks, just as Elizabeth had taught the Tibetans some Aramaic. Deborah also saw that Myrium and her son Jeshua would one day study at the monks' monastery in Tibet.

With tears in her eyes she said, "I remember dying in the arms of the beautiful being."

"Deborah," I said, "thank you for this extraordinary story. I'm ... I'm just stunned by what you've told me." I hesitated. *How could I say this?* I just plunged ahead. "I know you have dealt with this in your own work with clients, so I hope you won't take this wrong ... but ... can it be accurate? I mean, what do you think about a women's monastery? About that exchange of language and culture over enormous distances, so far back in time? About a student traveling to Tibet? Tibetan monks assisting at the time of the conception, and Jesus and Mary studying in Tibet? It is pretty mind-boggling, at least for my mind."

Deborah smiled and looked me directly in the eyes. Her voice was clear and confident. "Yes. I agree. It is far out. But it feels real to me—and why not? It seems plausible that it could have happened just like that. History isn't accurate, after all. Someone said, it's written by the winners. It's all about wars. This wasn't a war, but it certainly was a battle over a woman's right to revelation and serving God. I feel very proud of who I was. I feel even stronger, having relived my story today."

For days after this session with Deborah, I could not get Suddee out of my mind. She seemed to be such a monumental figure, a courageous agent of change. And yet she was nowhere to be found in history. Or so I thought. Though how could I say she was nowhere in history if I didn't do a little checking? With the ease of internet searches, there was no excuse not to do so. So I typed "Ancient Mount Carmel" into my search engine and discovered a few hints that Suddee and her monastery may have actually existed. A website owned by the Essene Nazarean Church of Mount Carmel, says, "In the middle of the second millennium B.C., the geographical lists of the Amin-Ra Temple at Karnak, the governing seat of Egyptian pharaohs, called this Carmel mount of the Essenes: 'the sacred promontory.' It was considered 'the most holy of all mountains and forbidden of access to many, according to Iamblichus, a Syrian Philosopher of the 4th century B.C.'

"Tradition also holds that the prophet Elijah had a vision of the future mother of Yeshua, and for this reason early Christians greatly honored him and Mount Carmel." The site further says, "There is even a Catholic Monastic Order, the Carmelites, who claim unbroken succession back to these ancient times."

This site included "Cayce Readings on Mount Carmel." I read it partly because I had never read any Edgar Cayce material before. The first lines to come up on the page gave me goose bumps: "Thus in Carmel—where there were the priests of this (Essene) faith—there were the (temple) maidens chosen who were dedicated to this purpose, this office, this service ... That was the beginning, that was the foundation of what ye term The Church."[5]

---

5. Essene Nazarean Church of Mount Carmel: http://www.essene.com/B'nai-Amen/carmelites.htm.

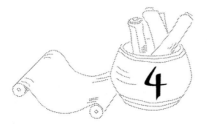

THE BROTHERHOOD

*A*round the same time I was working with Carol, I got a phone call from the popular Oregon psychic Laurie McQuary, inviting me to have coffee and meet her client Nick Bunick.

Laurie had seen very clearly that Nick had walked with the Master two thousand years ago, and she had been prompted by Spirit and her own Leo nature to prod Nick into doing what he'd come to do during this incarnation. Nick, a prominent and successful businessman, had said, "What am I supposed to do, get on the radio and say, 'Hi folks, I knew Jesus in a past life?' I'd look like an idiot!" He was frustrated with Laurie's insistence that he get on with it, because he didn't know what *it* was. He was, however, interested in learning more about this past life and decided to work with me. We had expected to have a session or two, but the work turned into thirteen sessions as we explored Nick's past life as the Apostle Paul in incredible detail. And, together with the help of G.W. Hardin, through our book, *The Messengers*, we presented not only Nick's personal spiritual journey but also his authentic telling of the story of Paul and his precious friendship with Jeshua.

Readers have told me that the book made the time of Christ come alive for them, that it made Jesus and Paul, Peter, Mark, and the other apostles accessible and human. One reader wrote: "Your book made them real people to me. It affirmed what I had always felt in my heart was true: that who Jesus was and what he intended has been very badly distorted almost from the beginning. I am so grateful to you, for bringing back Jesus' original messages and mission."

But readers and people attending my workshops and lectures have also had many questions: "Why now? Why are so many people having mystical experiences involving Jesus, the Mother Mary, and Mary Magdalene, at this particular time?" Many of these are people who, like myself, find some sects of the Christian religion lacking in spirituality, paralyzingly male-dominated, and full of judgment and fear.

"And what about the women?" they asked. "What about the women who knew Jesus? What roles did they play? Women aren't mentioned much in *The Messengers,* and the ones in the New Testament are usually watching from a distance—not part of the action."

This is hardly surprising since Yahweh, the God of the Hebrew culture from which came both the Old and New Testaments of the Bible, was depicted as utterly masculine. The authors of those texts believed that men were created in God's image and that the place of women was to serve them—except when cast in the role of luring them away from the good, the right, and the holy. "Where the God of Israel is characterized as husband and lover in the Old Testament," writer Elaine Pagels observed in her book *The Gnostic Gospels,* "his spouse is described as the community of Israel or the land of Israel."[6] In other words, the authors of these scriptural texts did conceptualize that God would have a spouse—they just could not seem to make his spouse a woman.

In recounting his past life as Saint Paul, Nick Bunick referred to Jesus' apostles as the Brotherhood. Was there a Sisterhood as well? In spite of persistent efforts to erase this possibility from

6. Elaine Pagels, *The Gnostic Gospels* (New York: Vintage Books, 1989), p. 163.

history (which started very, very early on and was entrenched by the fourth century) enough traces remain in recently recovered ancient documents and iconography for many scholars now to admit this view of women in early Christianity just may be true. Little Ruth insisted it was true. Paul, through Nick's recollections, was clear that women played an important part in the missionary effort after Jeshua's death—until there was trouble in the ranks.

Paul became distressed because a key member of his missionary team was having an affair. He said, "Some of these new officials are women, as well as men, and they're getting involved with each other carnally. So we have a serious situation to deal with ... Also, I don't think we should have women in those positions of responsibility because they're coming in too-close contact with the men."[7]

I asked, "What is the rule [you finally made] regarding women holding positions?"

"I won't appoint any more women. Women will no longer, as far as I'm concerned, hold positions of priesthood."

"Until then, what kind of positions were women holding?"

"The same as the men. There wasn't any deviation or selection based on gender."[8]

Much later, when Paul was in his sixties, I'd asked him about his attitude towards women (which some modern people consider misogynistic). He said, "That's not accurate [that he was against women]. My decision was based on prudence. We had too many incidents those first few years. And I made the decision based on what I felt was in the best interests of what we were trying to accomplish. It wasn't designed to discriminate against the women."[9]

I had, on a couple of occasions, asked Paul if he had spoken with Jeshua's mother. Had he ever asked her what she thought Jeshua would have wanted? He was aware of Myrium's where-abouts after Jeshua's death, but he hadn't consulted with her, nor had he even considered it.

7. Julia Ingram, G.W. Hardin, *The Messengers* (Lake Oswego: Skywin, 1996), p. 282.
8. Ibid, p. 283.
9. Ibid, p. 326.

It had been surprising to me that the women held positions equal to men early in the movement, given what history tells us about the Jewish practice of separating women and men during services and limiting study and leadership to men. However, Suddee, Ruth and many others I had yet to meet claimed that the Essene tradition to which Jeshua and Myrium belonged treated women and men equally. It wasn't a problem then. How did it become a problem later? Paul's reversal makes it even more understandable why the women had expected to serve as apostles and were furious when they were pushed aside.

THE QUEEN OF HEAVEN
IS DETHRONED

*I*n 1993, around Easter, several clients (not known to each other) reported scenes during regression hypnosis of being at Jesus' crucifixion. Like any transpersonal psychotherapist, I helped them to look at parts of their own current lives in which they experienced trial, death, and finally rebirth. These were powerful sessions, and it was easy for me to work with this material metaphorically. But, I had begun to wonder.

Why were images of Jesus and past-life regressions from that time in history suddenly making their appearances in the mind's eye of so many of my clients? Between the time that Carol and I worked with her memories of being Jeshua's sister and the publication of *The Messengers*, many dozens more of these clients appeared.

What was increasingly exciting and fascinating to me were the number of women who were claiming to have been disciples of Jeshua and even to have been his apostles. If women had been disciples and apostles along with the men, why was this not known? The Teachers, through Carol, had told me I had a spiritual assignment. If this information had been purposely obliterated from history, perhaps that had something to do with my assignment? Perhaps the time had come to restore a significant part of women's history and spiritual authority, as well as to answer the question about a Sisterhood.

I was eager to learn whether Mary Magdalene had reincarnated at this time, as had Paul and Ruth. If so, I prayed she'd find her way to me. The next person I met, however, was not Mary Magdalene but an equally significant Mary.

Hannah's was a familiar face around Portland's music scene. She performed in musical theater, gave voice lessons, and recorded a very beautiful cassette of children's lullabies. She was as comfortable singing in a synagogue or a Unitarian church as she was Christmas caroling at Saturday Market in Portland's historic Old Town. As a sound therapist, she used chanting, singing, and toning to help align the energies of her clients. When she was younger, she also served as a midwife. She's the type of woman we used to call an "earth mother." Everything she does is done with passion and good humor. We met while performing together in a musical-comedy number for a Unitarian church event. As we got to know one another, she said she'd like to do some past-life regression work with me.

Hannah is visually interesting. She's round-faced with large, expressive dark eyes. Her shoulder-length auburn hair is curly and flies freely. During our sessions, she frequently ran her fingers through her hair. And when she got really riled up, she pulled at it, shook it, as if her thoughts or feelings could fly out through the ends. She was uninhibited and noisy, sometimes singing or wailing. Unlike most clients, who are totally still during regressions, she moved around, gesturing, pointing, and crying out loud.

Before she went into trance, she explained that she had been feeling wracked with pain—a deep pain that she could not explain in her present life. She wanted to get to the core of this deep pain. She relaxed into my recliner, and as I began the hypnotic induction, tears rolled down her cheeks.

I prompted her. "Moving back in time now, letting your guides and teachers take you where you need to be. Three steps to go: three ... two ... one ... and out. Good ... good."

Hannah yawned. "I'm so tired."

"Why are you tired? What have you been doing?"

"Traveling [yawning and then sighing]. Traveling."

"Not enough sleep?" She sighed again, seeming about ready to fall asleep. "Are you traveling alone or ... ?" I didn't yet know who she was or what time period she was recalling.

"I just want to be somewhere comfortable." She started to cry. "It's early and it's not fair. I want to be somewhere comfortable."

"What is early?"

"The baby. The baby is early. The travel is bringing on labor ... and [still crying] I don't want to do this. I'm young ... [gasping for air] and ... "

"Scared?"

"And scared."

"Is there anyone there with you right now?"

"There's an ... angel [crying even harder than before]. And I'm holding on to him [showing relief]. It's Gabriel [a hysterical edge to the crying now]. He's using his trumpet to help me ... the sound comes down and out through here [pointing between her legs to the birth canal]. When it's time to push, there is a blast of his trumpet. He is assisting. He is birthing the baby through sound. This happens several times [sighing and smiling]. I'm feeling very little pain. He is making a shelter with his wings to protect us." She was quiet for several seconds, sighed deeply, and yawned again.

"Where are you? Will you describe your surroundings?"

"It's a cavelike space. Hollowed out. Straw. Joseph has made a bed of straw." Suddenly she clutched her belly in pain. "I've got to push! Joseph is here and ... Gabriel is here ... and ... "

"And you know you are going to be fine."

"Yes, I know I'm going to be fine. I just want it to be over. Gabriel holds me from behind, and Joseph is at my feet. He's out. He's born! Joseph knew what to do." She looked relieved, tired, and beautiful. "Jeshua [sighing and quietly weeping]. They are taking care of me. It's really wonderful. They are taking care of me. Gabriel is keeping watch."

This woman is reporting memories of having been the mother of Jesus. I wondered, Was this a metaphor for work Hannah needed to do or was it, in truth, a past life? How could we know? I asked more questions.

"Please tell me your name. Listen as your husband speaks your name."

"Myrium. He says, 'Myrium.'"

"Thank you, Myrium. And your baby ... you call him Jeshua?"

"As it was foretold." She appeared to be looking around, touched and weeping softly. "It is so wonderful that Joseph and Gabriel are taking care of me."

"Why shouldn't they?"

"They're men."

"Yes ... ?" At first I was confused.

"I thought I'd need to be with women."

"That was part of your panic?"

"I didn't need to be [afraid]. I'm so young, and I never gave birth before."

"And Joseph knew what to do."

"I feel extra safe with Joseph. He is not an ordinary man. He is a high priest ... involved with the mysteries."

"How old are you?"

"Fifteen."

"How's the baby?"

"He's beautiful [softly weeping]. He's beside me and warm. He is so beautiful. Gabriel's keeping people away. He's fluttering his wings [tears flowing again]. I want just to stay here for a while. Oh ... this is awful, though. We're to move because we are in danger. We have to be in the safety of our community in Alexandria. Joseph says the journey overland will take many days [crying harder, looking miserable]."

"You want to get back home?"

"I don't want to move. It's so hard. I'm bleeding and I feel itchy. I feel dirty and sweaty and itchy ... my legs feel like wood! A donkey! I'm sitting on a donkey trying to hold the baby and not fall. We have to go slowly [sobbing]. I just want to be home."

"Please move forward to a place where you are able to rest, and we will end this visit for now."

Over the next several weeks, Hannah returned for a dozen more regression sessions concerning her past-life memories as the mother of Jeshua. While we used this material as grist for the therapy mill—in other words, considering it metaphorically—she continued to feel that she was remembering an actual past life. At the end of one session, Hannah questioned how she could possibly claim this past-life identity? Was it about her ego? Was she just being dramatic and grandiose, or somehow just "making it all up"?

"In our culture," said Hannah, "Mary has been deified. How do I wade through the truth of it? How do I personally reconcile the way Mary is viewed now? What about those who claim to be having visions of her today? The statues crying blood tears? The manifestations?

"I guess," Hannah continued, "I have lots of different voices going on in my head. Part of me is saying, 'OK, I'm a highly creative person.'" She grinned at me. "I'm in the theater after all ... and I'm highly empathetic. I cry in movies. I mean I really get into the story. So is any of this real? What do I do with whatever this is, anyway?"

Like many others, she thought that everybody wants to believe they have been someone important in a past life. I reassured her that actually the opposite is true—most people are as worried as she was that they'll think they were someone famous.

"Well, these pictures that are coming up in my regressions don't necessarily match the biblical stories," said Hannah.

"Actually," I said, "they match the stories I've been hearing from clients."

"Really. Well, that makes me feel excited. But then there is another part of me that is going, 'Oh, great. Now what am I going to tell my friends? Hey, I was Mary in my past life.'" She laughed nervously, but with a bit of mischief in her eyes. "'Worship me. In fact, you should have been worshiping me all along!'"

She wiped her eyes with a tissue and shook her head, curls flying. "And then I thought back to how I was feeling the other day; it's like there's Myrium, this real person. But then, there's icon stuff. Statues of Mary. It bothers me a lot. I ask myself, is this what she wanted?"

I said, "I've met others with memories of that time, or what *seem* to be memories. And whether you're back physically—I mean reincarnated—and tapping into memories or accessing an archetype from that time, I have to say that something very powerful is happening. Not just to you, but to many people."

Archetypes, as defined by Gareth S. Hill in *Masculine and Feminine*, "are understood in Jungian psychology to be inborn patterns or forms for expectable, typical human experience."[10]

The word is derived from the Greek words *arch*, which means "origin," and *tupos*, which means "imprint." Even what might be thought of as universal archetypes, such as Mother and Father, are, however, in constant flux as they are defined and redefined over time and across cultures. Imagine how dynamic such archetypes as Hero, Savior, Lover, or Witch are. Ideas about what is heroic, for example, have been shifting from the ancient story of the completion of a transformational journey to its modern use of honoring someone who has died in service to others.

The names of real or mythical characters are symbols for a range of archetypes, great and small, and as disparate as Merlin (Wise Old Man); Peter Pan (Immature Male) and Wendy (Caregiver); Judas (Betrayer) and the Virgin Mary (Great Mother Goddess); or Wile E. Coyote (Eternal Fool). Each of these archetypes is shifting in meaning as humankind changes. Hannah was most definitely operating under the influence of Great Mother Goddess—but she was also contributing to her redefinition and her evolution.

These sessions with Hannah took place beginning in 1993, after Nick Bunick and I had already completed the first draft of *The Messengers*. I thought it would help her to read Nick's story because of the similar struggle he'd had in coming to grips with

10. Gareth S. Hill, *Masculine and Feminine* (Boston: Shambhala, 1992), p. xiv.

the realization that he had once lived as Paul the Apostle. So I loaned Hannah a copy of the manuscript.

Hannah called the next day and said she'd stayed up half the night reading and felt relief knowing someone else was having experiences similar to hers. She also said she felt upset with some of the things Paul had said. "Like, 'believe in Jeshua and you will be saved.' That wasn't right." I didn't say so then, but I didn't recall Paul ever saying that. It was interesting, though, that she had that perception.

At our next session, she told me, after considerable soul searching as well as talking things over with a couple of trusted friends, that she had decided she was ready to admit and accept her past-life memories were real. "I need to own her and all that having these experiences means," she said.

The following week, Hannah was back in the regression chair. As she began to breathe deeply, I asked, "Are you prepared now to return to the question which brought you to work with me in the first place?" Hannah nodded yes. "You said you were feeling deep grief. Shall we now go to the source of that deep grief?"

"The pain of the world. It feels very heavy. I feel deep grief. I feel hopeless about the way things are in the world. I thought we would succeed. But what happened after his death ... " She heaved a deep sigh.

"Has it been some time since Jeshua was murdered?"

"Yes, about twenty years."

"Did you feel this hopeless immediately after his death?"

"We had to retreat after it happened. We became more insular in what we were doing. People didn't understand. They weren't ready to understand. And so they saw what he did as magic, and they worshiped him because of the magic. That is off; that is wrong. After he was murdered, he came to me and told me to let it go. I felt such a conflict of emotion, because he was murdered!" She broke into sobs. "I didn't give birth to him for this [groans coming from deep in her chest]. Oh God! And the men aren't listening to me!" Her sobs grew louder.

"Take your time." I waited for her to grow quieter. She held out her hand for a tissue. I gave her a handful.

"I doubt that this work can go on without him being here. I don't think it's understood well enough yet. There are groups of followers who have different levels of understanding. But see, if there are twelve people, there are twelve different perspectives of how it should go out into the world. He was the hub of the wheel that kept the focus and the intensity and the power there. Put another way, say there are twelve notes in a scale. Jeshua was able to hold all the notes at the same time. There is no one else who is capable of doing that at this time, in that way." Sighing, she wiped the tears off her cheeks and blew her nose.

"Are there those in the present time—Hannah's time—who are capable?" I asked. "Or are you worried that this new effort is going to fail?"

"The time just wasn't right."

"But seeds were planted."

"Yes. Many, many seeds were planted. That's right. Maybe the seeds were planted for Hannah's time. I'm speaking for the present now. I'm seeing we have lived many lifetimes to get to this present day. I needed to live through many lifetimes to get what I needed in order to bring this to the present so it can flower now. It is time to move the populace to another level of existence, another level of *being*. Only it feels like everybody has come back now instead of salt and peppering. It's now becoming a groundswell to manifest a major shift in consciousness."

"You told me that Jeshua told his mother to let the past go, the present has great promise," I offered.

"Yes. The seeds were planted, and the work is growing. I feel that. But—and this is a very big 'but'—the men did not listen to Myrium, and she was Jeshua's mother. Nor did they listen to Mary Magdalene, and she was his wife and anointed successor. I wonder if we women will be listened to today?"

THE MANY MARY MAGDALENES

*A*fter Carol began channeling the Teachers, we decided to start a past-life study group. As destiny would have it, everyone who responded to my ad in the *Willamette Week*, and all those whom we subsequently drew to us, claimed past-life connections to the time of Christ. One of these women and one of these men told me of their strong connection to Mary Magdalene.

I worked with Jim first. He reported going immediately to Golgotha—and to the crucifixion of Christ. He wept during the entire session. His body was so wracked with grief, he couldn't speak. I wanted to help him, but it soon became obvious that this process of grieving was needed. It was moving that this man, while very masculine in appearance and behavior, was able to touch his feminine qualities so easily.

Tina appeared to "become" Mary during one of our group gatherings. She began speaking in a language none of us recognized but sounded vaguely like Arabic or Hebrew. We surmised it was Aramaic. It has been documented that regression clients do occasionally speak the language of the past life. It's

51

called *xenoglossia*. Because the meeting wasn't tape-recorded, we could not later have her words translated, so I don't know what she said. When I asked her to speak English, she immediately switched and asked to speak with Paul. Nick Bunick was in attendance that evening, so I invited him to come sit across from Tina. She identified herself as Mary, greeted him as an old friend and then proceeded to tell Paul off. She called him stubborn and expressed anger that he hadn't consulted with her about the organization following Jeshua's death and that he'd eliminated women from teaching roles. It was an aggressive dressing-down and I was a little concerned, but Nick was gracious and listened respectfully. Later, Nick said to me he didn't actually recognize the woman as having been Mary, but he didn't judge anyone else's experience. That remains true to this day. Nick blesses anyone who claims memories from that time.

What was interesting to me about the exchange that night was the assertiveness of the woman—her boldness and her anger. She said the same thing little Ruth had said, the same thing Hannah, the mother, had said: The women should have been included, consulted, taken seriously. And they weren't.

Shortly after the hardback version of *The Messengers* came out in 1997, my guides prompted me to hit the road. They told me several things: I needed more sunlight than was available in Portland; it was time to find a new home; there were people I needed to meet across the country; and I had unfinished business somewhere (to be revealed later). It seemed quite nuts to leave a busy private counseling practice at the height of the popularity and notoriety of *The Messengers*. However, the suggestion felt very right.

First, I gave my clients three months' notice that I was closing my practice. My long-term clients, some recovering from incredible childhood abuse and neglect, worked very hard during that time. I feel quite certain that I left no client feeling abandoned or that our work together was prematurely ended. In preparation for this unknown journey, I put all my belongings in storage, except for a reasonable selection of four seasons' worth of clothes, my laptop, cell phone, tape recorder, files, precious books, and inflatable kayak. All I knew as I closed the storage locker at exactly 4:44 P.M. was my first destination (of what was to become a one-year journey). I'd pleaded with my guides to tell me the outcome of this rather foolish-looking quest, but they had said, "It wouldn't be an adventure if you knew the ending, now would it?"

My first stop was in northwestern New Mexico at a writers' retreat. From there I went to Santa Fe to visit old friends, and then I was prompted to spend some time in beautiful, magical Taos. There, I met the next Mary Magdalene—the fifth of what would become dozens.

Thea and I met at a writers' workshop given by Taos resident Natalie Goldberg, who was promoting her latest book, *Living Color: A Writer Paints Her World*. Like me, Thea was passing through town and decided to stay a few days. We hit it off during the workshop and went for coffee afterwards. She asked if I was published, and I told her about *The Messengers*.

"Oh, my God!" she said. "Someone just gave me a copy. They sell it at the grocery store here. Did you know that?" I laughed. I didn't know that, but it seemed to be everywhere, even Costco. "I devoured it. It's true, isn't it? I know it is, and I feel like I was somehow a part of it."

I shrugged and smiled. "I have no doubt," I said, and then offered to regress her. It took us about five minutes to walk to the pretty little casita I'd rented in the heart of Taos.

Thea went into a very deep trance. She appeared dreamy and said she was sitting at her mother's knee. She identified herself as Mary.

I asked, "What's going on right now?"

"Mother is brushing my hair. I ask my mother, 'Why was I born?' She seems startled and says, 'What an odd question. You just are. It is one of God's mysteries why we are born.' I'm not satisfied with that answer. For many years, I've felt a sense of destiny. I have a calling, and I need to understand what it is."

"Go on," I prompted.

"The next day I ask my father the same question. He gives my question some thought and says it is one he's never asked himself. He will pray and ask God if we are allowed to know why anyone is born."

Mary said her father prayed earnestly for several days and one afternoon, while walking in his garden, he had a vision. He told Mary that in this vision he saw rows of wheat, ripe and ready for harvest. He was then shown the seeds from which the wheat had grown. Finally, he was shown the first seed. He then heard the words: "You and your family are like that first seed. You participated in the creation of man and woman. Just as wheat grows from the fruit of itself, so do humans. There are many varieties of wheat, so are there many varieties of humans. The reason wheat reproduces itself is simple. Underlying all life is the creative urge to recreate itself. There is consciousness in all living things. Human consciousness informs the mind and body to change and grow with experience. You and your family [the soul family] are among the millions of souls who are invested in manifesting pure creative energy while in human form. This means living through the heart to love all beings as one's own creations." Mary beamed as she continued this monologue as if she were right there, repeating her father's words.

"Your human family has chosen to be together at this time to participate in a leap forward toward that end. There *will be an end* of fearing each other and an embracing of loving one another. Each of your children will play a part in the shifting of beliefs. Your part of this as father is to encourage your children to think for themselves—the girls especially. Teach Ruth, Mary, and Martha what you teach your son, Lazarus, and emphasize independent thought. Encourage them to pray for answers, just as you have done today. Answers will come to them, not through their priests or other teachers, but through their own God Source."

I asked Mary, "How is this remarkable vision received by the family?"

"Mother's first reaction is to be afraid. She isn't used to having her husband discuss matters of God with her or us girls. She was taught that her role was to support her husband while he studies the Scriptures and talks to God. But father persists, and we pray together."

"Please move forward to the next significant event," I prompted.

"Joseph and Myrium have come to Bethany to visit. At our evening meal, my father decides to tell Joseph and Myrium about what he heard and saw in the garden. Father tells me to sit beside him and listen. Joseph is very moved and says he's honored that he's considered a close enough friend to be trusted. Then Joseph says, 'As you know, sixteen years ago, I was visited by a radiant being who talked to me about my mission and about the mission of our son Jeshua. I was told that Myrium would give birth to the Anointed One and that I was to love and support them both.'

"My mother asks Myrium if she has visions, too. Joseph laughs and says, 'She speaks with angels every day and often has messages for me.'"

"What are you making of all this, Mary?" I asked.

"I knew Jeshua was the Anointed One. He is almost fifteen and knows for certain why he has been born. He's a friend, too. We've played together for years."

"What happens next?"

"The men are excited as they discuss the importance of what is happening to them and to their families."

"Did Jeshua come to Bethany with his parents today?"

"No, he isn't here. I'm not sure where he is."

"Do you learn more about your own destiny?"

"My father says he doesn't know specifically what my part is, but because I was the one to ask the question he thought it would be significant."

"Move forward again."

"My father calls me into the garden and tells me it's time for me to begin my instruction and that I am to go, along with Ruth, to Mount Carmel. Ruth is getting married in a few weeks, but she really wants to go. To tell the truth, I don't think she wants to get married. Her betrothed isn't very interested in spiritual matters. I think he's boring."

Mary began her studies at age twelve. She spent several months at Mount Carmel on three different occasions. Myrium taught her and several other girls about energy centers in the body, the chanting of ancient Sanskrit words, and other mysteries not even revealed to her father. Mary's mother died of a high fever shortly after Mary turned fifteen. Her father died not long afterwards.

Mary wept at the death of her father. "He said that he would stay nearby to assist his daughters and his son, because many trials lay ahead."

I asked Mary to describe her studies at Mount Carmel in more detail.

"I have two main teachers. Myrium teaches chanting, meditation, astral travel, and how the vibrational properties of sound, color, and fragrances (flowers and oils) aid in healing. My other teacher is Judith. From her, I'm learning ancient temple rituals passed down in the Greek and Jewish traditions—chanting, prayer, creating beautiful spaces using flowers, fragrance, music, and color, and interpreting astrological signs."

"Judith says I'm a natural teacher, healer, and visionary." She blushed. "I'm thinking about becoming a teacher here, and Myrium tells me I'll be a teacher someday, but for now I must return to Bethany to be with Lazarus and Martha. When I'm a little older, I will be instructed in the art of tantra."

The session had gone on for almost three hours and we were both tired, so I brought it to an end. I hoped to get more information from Thea, but she had to leave Taos and get back to work. She laughed and said, "I think you'll be amused to know what I do for a living: I teach tantric yoga and run workshops on tantric sexuality."

Looking back on my meeting with Thea, I realized that many of the women I had met or would meet after Taos, who reported Mary Madgalene's story, were not only deeply spiritual but sensual.

How puzzling that more than one person could claim they had been Mary—or Ruth, or Peter, for that matter—in a past life. Was this wishful thinking on their parts? Was the process of rebirth more complicated than we've been led to believe? Or was there another explanation? These people I'd met had nothing to gain by confabulating a story. Nick Bunick had fielded that particular question a few times. Had he just made up the story that he had been Paul in a past life? Nick said to the skeptics, "It doesn't make any sense that I'd pay Julia for thirteen sessions to sit in her chair with my eyes closed and make up a story. What would be the point of that?" When someone accused him of just wanting notoriety or perhaps financial gain, Nick laughed. He had risked everything to go public with his story—his wealth, his reputation, and his close relationships. I was certain of one thing: People were not making up these stories. I had more questions than answers about how the process worked, however—and *why*.

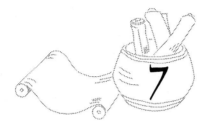

The Messiah's
Kindergarten Teacher

*W*hile in Taos, I decided it was time for me to start the book about the Sisterhood, so I spent the next several days transcribing tapes of sessions that clients had given me permission to duplicate. Among the tapes were several sessions with a woman I'll call Anna. She and I met in the early 1990s when she joined the past-life study group. She is a colorful woman. She dances like the island girl she is, wild and sensual. She has a loud, infectious laugh, but also has a serious, mystical side. Born and raised in the Caribbean as a Catholic, she later studied Buddhism. Anna has been an inspiration to me because of the courageous way she follows her own spiritual advice.

She reported a lifetime as a teacher living in the same Essene community as Myrium, Jeshua's mother. She told me she was fifteen years old and that her name was Anarisa. During the regression session, she spoke in a soft and gentle manner, almost whispering.

"I'm surrounded by children, and they are happy to be with me. My guides said to tell you I'm wearing a blue robe."

I asked, "What is the significance of your blue robe?"

"I wear the blue robe of an initiate teacher. I need only one more year of training to be called Teacher."

"Your pupils—are they boys, girls, or both?"

"Yes, both."

"And how old are your pupils?"

She giggled. "Some few are three; most of them are four, five and six; a few of them are seven and eight—two of them."

"What's today's lesson?" She chuckled with glee at the scene in her mind's eye.

"How to use energy to bounce your ball. And how to fly."

Some of the most interesting information can come through past-life sessions. "I'd like to watch you while you teach. Please go ahead."

"Hmm. I have to get situated."

"Take your time."

"It is the beginning of the day." She laughed affectionately. "They are so excited. I have a ball. My guides are telling me to tell you what it is made of."

"And what is it made of?"

"Resin?" It was as if Anna were surprised at what Anarisa had said.

"Resin. A resin ball," I said.

"Yes. And it has some cloth on it, too. I have it on the table that faces the children. As I walk toward the table, I am making the ball rise."

"And how are you doing that?"

"Through my spiritual eye. I send an energy beam that ... dislocates?" She frowned. "No ... "

She seemed to be listening for the right word. It appeared that Anna was translating Anarisa's experience into English.

"That might be it. Go on," I prompted.

"Dislocates the molecules of the ball. Even though the ball does not lose its shape, it frees up enough of the molecular structure that it will levitate through the use of my energy beam. It is easier to do than to explain."

I laughed. "Who taught you?"

"It seems to me I have always known. They [her guides] want me to tell you I was in school just like these children. But I started when I was two years old."

"Go on. What happens next?"

"One of the three-year-olds wants to make the ball levitate. He is so excited. It makes me feel good when they can do it. It means they understand. He will be another who will teach." A look of immense love came over Anarisa's face, and she began to weep. "Excuse me for my emotions."

"Who is this little boy?" She whispered something I couldn't hear.

"I'm deciding if ... I ... can tell you. They say I can. It's very hard for me to tell you."

"Your information is safe with me. I promise you."

"I understand." She took a huge breath. "I am to tell you that in this class ... at this time ... the little boy who I teach ... "

"Yes?"

"His name is Jeshua [sweetly], and I love him very much. He honors me by being my student. Although all my children honor me. Please safeguard that information. It is important, but I trust you."

I matched her gentle tone. "Thank you. I know quite a bit about Jeshua."

"It seems you would if you are from where this body's from ... "

"Yes, your future."

"Yes, we know. It's interesting. I've been waiting to share this information, but it's hard sometimes."

"I've heard that your community has secrets it needs to guard from those who might misuse the information."

"We don't want to be different, but we are."

"Do all of your students live here?" I asked.

"Yes."

"And what is the name of this place?"

"I have been given permission. She [meaning Anna, her present-life self] will be able to tell you by a map." Later, she pointed to the location of Mount Carmel, in the Holy Land.

"OK. Thank you."

"You're welcome."

"You said earlier that you were also teaching flying. Would you explain how you teach flying?" Little Ruth had spoken of learning to fly. I found it interesting that they both used that term.

She chuckled and seemed very amused. "I'm trying to convey to them the ... ooooh ... big word ... intricak, no ... intricacies?"

"Yes, intricacies."

"Hum."

"You are doing very well translating. So you are teaching the intricacies of astral projection."

"Correct. Translating is simple because the person [Anna] knows many languages." She took a deep breath and appeared to be accessing information. "Wait. The number-one lesson is not to fear. If they are afraid, the body will become very heavy." She appeared to be giving a lecture. "If you do not experience fear, the body will remain flexible, open, for the spirit to easily project. When fear occurs, it affects all levels of what we will call your body. Do you understand?"

I said, "I know the feeling of being heavy with fear, yes."

"Your body is composed of the physical body and the astral body. Fear constricts both the astral and physical body. Because you fear in the third dimension, it will transpire ... yes, transpire—good word—transpire through the other dimensions, making it difficult to fully expand into other dimensions. Do you understand?"

"Yes. So you are teaching the children, first of all, this is not to be feared. Where are you going today?"

"We are going to see planets. The children are to get specific information which they will then share. It is what you call a field trip, even though we aren't physically going anywhere. I make sure that all of them are OK. I follow them. I give them two planets to look at—Jupiter and the one next to Saturn, Uranus. Some of the children are enjoying the rings and go through the gases. There are some I see retreating, so I go and envelop them. They are scared, but they go. Time spent is no more than fifteen minutes. The children are really excited upon return."

"I have a question for you, Anarisa. It sounds as if this is something everyone in your community is able to do. What is the value?"

"Interesting question. Don't you know?"

"I have some ideas, but would like to hear yours."

"It is important for us to maintain our connection with all the dimensions. This ability reduces the effects of the third dimension of physicality. It allows us to remain very connected with all that is. God is in everything. We experience God in all that is. Those who don't know believe they are alone. One of the aspects of physical reality is to forget. When I astral project, it minimizes the disconnection."

"Thank you. That was a beautiful explanation. Please move forward to another event in your role as Jeshua's teacher." She took a deep breath.

"Yes. He is a young man now. He has just returned from the East and is feeling depressed. He misses the calmness of the monastery where he had learned so much. Back here, in our Essene village, he is aware of what lies ahead. He comes to me for guidance."

"And what is your guidance, Anarisa?"

"We explore his heart. He is young, and the full force of what lies ahead is dawning on him. He needs to play a little, feed his soul with the things he loves, and forget himself for a time. Alexandria is a place where he can do that. He will go there. Imbalance adds to depression, so I also prescribe dancing. Moving to music engages specific chakras and brings the body back into balance. I dance with Jeshua both physically and energetically." She smiled broadly and laughed. "Now he is laughing again. It comes from the deepest part of him. When he laughs, it is contagious. In Alexandria, he will study astronomy, which is his passion. He likes seeing the universe from a different perspective, and it will help him to navigate his astral trips. He will also study philosophy, music, and art. He loves to feast his eyes on paintings and sculptures. Like me, he can feel the creative energy of the artist when he looks at art. But I remind him that he needs to spend time with friends most of all."

"Thank you. Will you now please look forward into your own future, Anarisa, and tell us how long you taught. Did you teach all of your life?"

"Yes. They want me to tell you that I was teaching from the time I was ... six?... until I was, hmm, fifty-six [deep breath] ... Yes, that is correct."

"And how old are you at your death?"

"Sixty-three."

"Did you teach other things besides working with energy?"

"Well ... everything is energy, so to answer your question, yes, I taught everything [laughing gently]. I taught all that is related to energy. I taught how to use it to heal. How to use it to repair fields. Body energy fields. My energy work was all encompassing in regards to the body. Does that answer your question?"

"Yes, thank you. Will you now move forward to near the end of that life?"

"It's been many years since Jeshua was killed. We became more protective. People outside became more hostile towards us. Our community continued its work. There was more activity towards safeguarding information. Because, as you well know, humanity has free will [sniffles], and even though we know our future, as well as our present and our past, there is never a certainty. Things can change. So we safeguarded our knowledge."

"How did you safeguard it? What are some precautions you took?"

She took a deep breath. "We hid teachings."

"Hid them?"

"We made sure people had the knowledge memorized. But more."

"Did you have soldiers? Did you have to defend your community against attack?"

"We had two scares. They were very close [whispering], very close. Interesting. I did feel some fear then. We did have two scares. But was there a third? I must be blocking. Wait. Hmm. Should I tell you?"

"Yes, please."

"I have been prepared for this. Excuse me for my emotions. I was in my living quarters. My husband had died. The people were scurrying around."

"Oh, dear." I knew what was coming and I felt as upset as she must have that this peaceful, loving community was about to be destroyed.

"We all knew [sniff] ... we all knew this was not a scare. This was a reality. They were coming, and we would be killed. Even after all the teachings, even after all the understanding I have about physical death and what it means, I was still happy with the fact that my children were not there. They were traveling, and I [weeping] would die alone. But, that was all right. They were safe. I completed the work I came here for. I had done everything I needed to do. The teachings would either move on, or they would perish, but I had done the best I could. They came through our secret doors. We thought there had been a spy."

"Oh. A spy gave away the secret?"

"But we had [sigh] ... we all knew ... and we all died."

"Oh," I said, whispering. "I'm so sorry."

It was time to draw the day's session to a close. I felt incredible affection for this sweet, brave woman and deep grief that she and everyone in her community had been killed. I brought Anna out of the trance with a post-hypnotic suggestion not to bring back any of the pain or fear of what happened to Anarisa's body. I said, "Anarisa was so sweet. Such manners. I could learn from her."

Anna blew her nose and laughed and said, "Me too!" I looked at Anna with new respect. I wasn't ready for her to leave, and she wanted to process the session, so we talked.

"Spiritual teachers frequently say we have forgotten who we are and that our task is simply to ... remember," I said. "I used to feel annoyed by that statement. Who am I? I'm Julia: five-foot-eleven, blue eyes, auburn hair, now turned white ... mother, therapist, teacher, friend, activist ... sometimes sweet, sometimes hostile, sometimes generous, at other times jealous. A human being. That's part of who I think I am in my physical body. What is it that I forget?

"But Anarisa helps us to understand what those spiritual teachers mean. Who we are is God: one of the countless millions of souls that make up what we call creation. But, as I live in this body, with my distinct present-life personality and with my limited ability to view the total picture with my brain, I have a hard time remembering I am God."

Anna nodded agreement. "Anarisa said that those who don't know how to remind themselves feel disconnected from their own God-self and believe they are alone."

When we maintain our connection to the All, through all of the dimensions, it reduces the effects of being in a physical state or, as Anarisa put it, "It minimizes the disconnection." The way Anarisa stayed connected was to travel astrally. Some people today have that ability. Many people remind themselves through meditation and yoga, others through prayer. Because I use self-hypnosis easily, I connect to the dimensions through that altered state. I still forget sometimes, especially when I allow fear to creep into my thoughts and feelings. But, when I remind myself by going back into that place of connection, I remember that my God-self is a constant force, a burning sun.

MYRIUM AND JESHUA IN TIBET

*D*uring one of Hannah's sessions, reporting her lifetime as Myrium, she dropped a small hint as to where Jeshua/Jesus went during what's been termed "the lost years."

"Are there flowers in here?" She meant, did I have fresh flowers in my office?

"No."

"I'm smelling flowers [sniffing the air]. It's strong ... really fragrant."

"Where are the flowers?" I asked, pulling her back into the past.

"Oh. It is Jeshua's birthday. We've decorated the room— flowers everywhere. He's really excited and ... I'm feeling sad [laughing nervously]. I know now's the time he starts his education, and it will take him away [bursting into tears]. I love him so much. He's very sweet."

"Does he know yet?"

"That he's going away? I don't think he does. See, it's hard with him to know what he knows. He knows things in a deep ... he knows things. But he's still a little boy, and there are times when I don't know which part is operating." She laughed out loud.

"What are you remembering?"

"He's just so cute the way he plays with the other children. They're dancing with each other. They're celebrating. There's music. Jeshua's turning seven today. It's an important age for boys because that's when they start their education. His education's going to be different. Some will be the same as the other boys, and some will be different. Some of it will be far away." She sighed and looked sad.

"Will you go with him some of the time?"

"Yes, I've been told that I will travel with Jeshua from time to time over the years. My education will continue, just as his is beginning."

Myrium explained that, along with his education and training in Capernaum, Jeshua would also go to Mount Carmel to study with other Essene masters. "Another woman I'm working with," I said, "mentioned Mount Carmel. She said she watched Jeshua, who was about seventeen, move a coin from one hand to another by using his energy and intention."

"Yes, that must have been my daughter, Ruth. She was there at times when Jeshua was there."

I smiled to myself. It was little Ruth who had told me about the coin. When one person mentions something another has reported, especially when they don't know each other, there's a sense of validation. Not that I've ever felt the point of all of this was to rewrite history. I have no intention of doing that because it isn't possible to back up by objective evidence all of what my regression subjects have reported. Still, when the same information comes from independent reports, I'm inclined to take it even more seriously.

"And then when he turns thirteen or fourteen, he'll be old enough to study in our community in Alexandria," Myrium continued.

"Would you move forward to a time when you went with Jeshua to one of his training locations abroad?" I prompted.

She nodded and took a deep breath. She moved her head from side to side, as if looking around to get her bearings. Finally, she spoke.

"Well, I think we're somewhere in Tibet. The room is large and cavernous. I'm walking down a hallway and I see tonkas [woven banners]. One tonka. It's actually very sparse. Simple material helps simplify the mind. There are Sanskrit shlokas. Our teacher is saying, 'Nada Brahma.'[11] He's talking about kundalini energy."

Suddenly, I felt myself slipping into an altered state myself. This was not the usual state I reach as I entrain or connect vibrationally with clients, but much deeper. I struggled to pull myself out of that hallway Hannah was describing so I could focus on her. I shook my head and took a drink of water. "What else are you learning?" I finally asked.

"That Sanskrit's a very important language. You can spin your chakras through Sanskrit syllables. Then there are shlokas—chants. We spend a lot of time meditating. He gives us practices. Then we go back to him and talk about what we experience, and he gives us more, and we do more. It's very powerful."

"Please move forward to the most significant experience here."

"Well, Jeshua's twitching and I am too [sighing]. It's like an explosion going off in the body. It's like fireworks that rise from the bottom and go up and explode at the top. We're taking that energy and running it. Breathing ... that's the energy we run when we heal others. Oh my God!"

"What is happening now?"

"I'm feeling this energy. There's something I need to say. When we run this energy through our bodies we raise the energy level. Chanting in Sanskrit helps with the resonance. It is a tool. We each make individual adjustments." She had been yawning throughout this session.

"Why does the body need to yawn so much today?"

"Because this is really exhausting, all this sitting and focusing inside, and I'm just getting sick of it [laughing heartily]. I need to get outside and smell something. It's very different from home. It's harsh in many ways. Stark and harsh. Sitting for long hours of meditation. And the food—very plain. I'm so bored with barley."

"How long have you been here?"

11. "The world is sound" or "Sound is God, Creator of the universe."

"Forever. [Laughs] Ugh! I miss home and my children. Ruth is still little [weeping now]. I'm feeling really human right now."

"How much longer do you need to stay?"

"A few more weeks. Jeshua is drinking all this up like a sponge. He's like a vessel. All this just needs to be poured into him. We can't go until he's finished."

"You are doing this for his sake?" I knew she was. I actually felt like I knew a great deal about how she felt and what Jeshua was learning.

"I'd do anything for him. I love him so much. [Crying hard] I'm at the end of what I can take in, so now I sacrifice and wait. But I'm yearning to go home."

"It's such a long journey," I said. She told me later about stops they made in India and China on their way to Tibet. However, the major teaching took place there at the monastery. "I speak to Jeshua about the sacrifices we have to make."

"What does he say?" I asked.

"It's for the greatest love. For love that's greater than anything we've ever known."

"Do you understand?"

"I feel it in my heart, but it's a paradox. Why do I feel the pain? It's reciprocity, pain and suffering, caring and love. It all comes from here, from the heart. We must feel pain and suffering in the world in order to feel all the love in the world. It's a big circle in the heart." She shook her head and ran her fingers through her curly hair. "I have to move! I need to dance and walk and smell something good."

I prompted her to move forward to a time when she did just that.

"I like the people so much. I like to explore the village and discover the culture. I'm walking in the streets now. I see lots of red color—fabrics, colorful fabrics. Texture. Embroidery. It's very pretty. This is where the life is! I hear music. Someone's blowing a horn. The laughter of children playing. And the smells [sniffing]— very flavorful. People seem happy and alive. They walk a lot. There are rocks, things made of rocks; their homes are made of rocks. There are piles of rocks everywhere! Oy! The air is very thin, and I'm getting tired."

It was time to end the session. After Hannah left, I sat in silence for several minutes. I had gone more deeply into her experience than I had with any client or in any session. I *knew* that hallway Myrium had described. I needed to know why this session hit me so deeply. I called Nick Bunick and asked him to regress me. He agreed to help me and suggested that G.W. Hardin sit in on the session and ask questions if he felt moved to do so.

He Who Watches Over Spirit

I felt it was important that Nick facilitate my regression session and that G.W. be a witness, and I was grateful they had agreed. Just like many of my clients, I was excited and nervous as I sat in the recliner, wondering if I would be able to successfully discover the source of my strong feelings about the Tibetan monastery Myrium had described. Nick's hypnotic induction is different from mine but it worked equally well. Nick prompted my high self to take me back to that time when I had known the hallway that Myrium had described in her session.

I saw myself as a male in that lifetime, introduced to a monastery (I later said it was in the city of Leh) at age three and then delivered by my parents at age seven. At twelve, I was given the name He Who Watches Over Spirit, and was told by my teacher that I had served "the All" for many lifetimes. At this point in the session, I had not yet learned that this was during the time of Christ.

"My teacher makes me feel the bigness of the name; when I am with him I expand. There are certain of us who come from dimensions of light, who have chosen to be the bringers of light, keepers of the spirit on this plane."

"Please move forward into a future significant event," Nick said.

"I am now thirty years old. I have succeeded at certain tasks that were presented to me. I can now enter into study of the secret teachings. It is not a competition at all; it is simply a matter of gaining understanding and having the discipline to go further. There are three of us [who have moved to the first level of study]. There are three levels of mastery within the sacred teachings, which take place in rooms below the monastery."

"Say more about mastery," Nick prompted. However, I didn't comply.

"At age fifty-one I mastered level two. I'm now fifty-two, and I've been assigned to work with a special pupil, one some call 'Issah,' but whom I call 'Ya-swa.' He, his mother, and his cousin have just arrived in Leh." I reported that, in her youth, Myrium had been instructed by monks who had traveled to Mount Carmel to help her in preparing Jeshua. She introduced her son and his cousin John (John the Baptist) to the monastery in Tibet.

Nick asked, "What is it like to be one of Jeshua's teachers?"

"*Teach* is not quite the word. He is an enlightened one. It is as if the information is already there; one need but touch him and the knowledge is there. We are simply providing space for him to remember."

"Would you please describe your pupil?"

"He is a boy. His skin is much lighter than ours. Light eyes. Golden, brownish hair. Darker brown with the gold. He is about the same height as I. He is so sweet. He is a sweet, gentle boy. He learns quickly and has a good sense of humor. He has a graceful body. His mother taught him enough of our language that he gets by. But much of our communication is nonverbal."

"What is his cousin like?"

"John is a puzzle. He is curious and eager to learn, but he is very undisciplined. He is loud and a jokester. He dislikes meditation. John was encouraged to return to his home."

"Could you give more details about the teaching?"

"In the bowels of this monastery there is a room where the initiated go and where the sacred writings are stored. Here we are trained to move into other dimensions where we receive more training. We physically move [bi-location, in contrast to astral travel]. Jeshua will be taught this. He will be taught to manifest physical objects. He can already elevate above his body. He will be taught to transport his body from here to Qumran [the Essene monastery near the Dead Sea]. He will be taught to heal."

I reported that Jeshua remained in the Leh monastery two years and completed the first level of training. Several years later, he came back to continue his studies. The second time, he came alone.

"He is taller. Now, he has a beard, his hair is longer. Personally, he is not as shy. *Shy* is not the right word ... he is more confident."

"Has Jeshua shared his mission with you?"

"We knew before he came. He is a master. He is a master of the stature of the many Buddhas, gods, and goddesses. This is the first time a master has been born in the area of the Dead Sea. He is to bring the teachings to that part of the world; to build upon the knowledge that is already there; to continue that which has already been started. He was born to that region for that purpose. His people had Scripture and tradition that had prepared his community for his birth. He was expected."

"Do you have knowledge of what happened to Jeshua as he returned home, and especially when he himself began teaching?"

"Yes. The people of his area were not like us. They were not as hungry or as spiritual, not as curious; they were not receptive. He was discouraged. But, as the teaching progressed and he began to demonstrate his ability, he caught the attention of the people. More and more began to listen. The most important teaching is that which we all know: God is one God; God is within; God is everywhere. God is love."

"You yourself achieved the third level of initiation, is that correct?"

"Yes."

"Will you tell us some of what you were taught?"

"I am able to change my body, the molecules in my body. I can be in two places at once. I can boil water with the heat of my hands. I can elevate my body; I can heal with my touch, with my words; I can move to other dimensions and other solar systems. I can interpret the spiritual symbols from the scrolls." He Who Watches Over Spirit taught Jeshua from scrolls which contained hologram-like symbols. They were beautiful beyond description.

"Did Jeshua complete his studies?" asked Nick.

I sighed. "No, he was murdered before he could return a third time."

One of the questions G.W. had, once I came out of trance, was the location of the monastery I'd reported. I'd said *Le* (pronounced *lay*). He hadn't heard of it and thought it was too simple a word to be Tibetan. However, we did a little research and found there is a small Himalayan city called Leh, which is in the Ladakh region (which I did know about thanks to having read Andrew Harvey's book *A Journey in Ladakh* (Houghton Mifflin, 1983) many years ago). It is in India near the modern border of Tibet. Historically, it was part of the vast Indian empire which later became part of Tibet. The Silk Route ran through Leh, which was validating to me because it was a little hard to imagine Mary, Jesus, and John making a journey into the Himalayas two thousand years ago when it's hard to get there today except by air. I now understood it was plausible that they had traveled with merchants.

I thought I had been a Buddhist monk, although I didn't specifically say that. I doubted, however, that my information could have been factual as I believed that Buddhism hadn't traveled from southern India into that region until two or three hundred years after Jeshua's death. However, research revealed that the territory which includes modern Ladakh was part of the enormous empire of Ashoka the Great, an empire which stretched from modern Afghanistan across Kashmir and included Nepal and most of the Indian subcontinent. It was said that Ashoka was horrified by the carnage of a bloody war to unite India and became a follower of the teachings of the Buddha. He renounced war and conquest and translated Buddhist teachings into government policy. He brought Buddhism to the area of Ladakh in the third century B.C.

A friend of mine, Dr. Walter Semkiw, author of *Return of the Revolutionaries* (Hampton Roads, 2003), believes that souls evolve linearly. He is skeptical of anyone who reports a past life of great talent or wisdom but who doesn't display those same gifts, or more, in the current lifetime. If Walter is correct, then I should be able to do everything that He Who Watches Over Spirit could do, and more.

A Buddhist teacher in Tucson, Gen Kelsang Lingpur, says of reincarnation that we think in terms of lives in a straight line, but in fact there is no such thing as time on the spiritual plane.

I had gotten that same information during my first regression in the mid-1980s (with the man I'd called Santa Claus). When I was in that space between lives and viewed the records of my own lifetimes, I saw those records as scrolls set into the walls of a circular building. I could visit my so-called past, present, or future. I knew then that our spiritual evolution is not linear. That remains my belief, and Walter and I have agreed to disagree on that point. The dozens of my own so-called past lives with which I have worked include lifetimes of great joy and high spiritual functioning, but I've also seen myself in lifetimes when I was a tyrant, a ruthless soldier, a cruel sea captain, a liar, and a thief. When lined up chronologically, there is no pattern of evolution, or de-evolution. When viewed from my records room, however, I see that I am—by my acts today and every day—influencing all of my lifetimes, for better or worse. I take great joy in knowing that within my spiritual DNA resides a monk who can change his molecules. Obviously, that is not my main focus or purpose in this incarnation as Julia, but I'm working on it anyway.

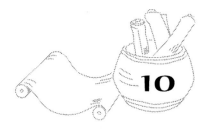

RUTH MONTGOMERY

*T*he tape recorder clicked off as the recording of my past-life regression as a monk came to an end. I'd only been gone from Portland three weeks, but already I missed my friends and family. Listening to Nick and G.W.'s voices again made me sad and lonely. Worse, it made me wonder if leaving home had been impulsive and foolish. *No turning back now, though,* I thought. It was time to take a break and stretch my body. I headed down to the coffee shop where I'd become a regular, sipped a latte, and watched a spectacular high desert sunset.

I enjoyed my time in Taos. There, I had my first hot stone massage, saw my first strawbale house mudding party, and visited the sustainable homes called earthships. Of course I visited the Taos Pueblo and the many art shops and museums that make this quirky community so interesting.

The fourth week after I'd left Portland, I got a call from Nick. He said Ruth Montgomery was looking for me. Ruth had honored us by endorsing *The Messengers*, an honor she never gave to another book before or after. I felt as if I'd been summoned by a master teacher and called her immediately. She told me that after she'd read our book, she'd become aware of how many of her close friends in the southern Florida community in which she lived were reincarnated Essenes. She asked if there was any chance I could come to regress a few of them.

"Any chance?" I nearly shrieked. "I'm in New Mexico now and free to travel. In fact I'm going wherever Spirit moves me or wherever I'm invited."

"Consider yourself invited to Florida," Ruth said. She gave me the name and number of her good friend who would handle all the arrangements, and we agreed on a tentative date about a month ahead. Since I'd be going cross-country, I wanted to visit Carlsbad Caverns, my son in Tulsa, a friend in Kansas City, and just for fun, get to Florida by way of New Orleans—a place I'd always wanted to experience. I timed the New Orleans visit to coincide with the full moon so I could stand on Bourbon Street and sing along with Sting.

After two and a half weeks in Taos, I was back on the road. I love caves and spent a full day exploring Carlsbad—a spiritual experience in itself. My time with my son was a happy reunion. I enjoyed visiting the campus where he was studying to be a minister of music. Tulsa impressed me as a very pretty city, with its many parks and bicycle paths. From Tulsa I went to Kansas City and spent a few days with a friend who reported a beautiful past life as Anne, one of the Sisterhood. Her story appears later in the book. My arrival in Naples, Florida, in mid-October was perfect, for the humidity was low and the temperatures moderate.

I often refer to Ruth Montgomery as the Mother of Modern Metaphysics. She has been ranked with Nostradamus and Edgar Cayce for her great powers of foresight. A past president of the National Press Club, she began her writing career as a political reporter. The morning I spent with her in her penthouse apartment, she showed me a wall entirely covered with photographs of her with several presidents, first ladies, and members of Congress.

After meeting Jeane Dixon, the famous psychic who had warned President Kennedy not to go to Dallas the day he was shot,

Ruth wrote the book *A Gift of Prophecy* (William Morrow, 1965). She then dove head first into researching the world of the paranormal. When her good friend Arthur Ford died and began speaking to her from the other side, her destiny was clear. Ruth told me she would simply place her hands on her typewriter keys and her fingers would move automatically. That automatic writing yielded fifteen books.

It was my good fortune that Ruth celebrated her eighty-fifth birthday while I was visiting, and I got to attend the dinner party given in her honor. It was wonderful for all of us women to be able to share with her what an impact she'd had on our lives.

Ruth's young friend, who I'll call Sarah, handled all the details of my Naples visit. She arranged for me to stay in nice places and put out the word that I was in town. She managed my schedule and made me feel like a member of the family. Among the many delights of my almost three weeks in Naples were the number of reincarnated Essenes with whom I was privileged to work. Of course, I already knew that Ruth Montgomery had been another Ruth, the older sister of Lazarus, Mary, and Martha, because I'd read the account in her book *Companions Along the Way* (Fawcett Books, 1991). She hoped to get more information about that lifetime. I was in for a treat here in Florida, as I was to meet Ruth's whole spiritual family from that time, including Lazarus, Martha, Mary, Sarah (daughter of Joseph of Arimathea), and others from that time.

On my first night in Naples, Sarah had Ruth and me over for dinner so we could meet each other. Ruth reiterated that her guides had confirmed that Nick Bunick had indeed been Paul in a past life. She said her guides had told her that I had been a part of that movement, too. I thanked her warmly for the confirmation and for her invitation to meet her ancient family. Eventually, the discussion got around to Mary Magdalene. Ruth said, "I get so many letters from women who say they were Mary Magdalene." Grateful for the opening, I told her the same thing was happening to me and asked what she thought about the phenomenon. She answered, "It can't be. There can be only one person who was

Mary." We had other things to discuss, so I didn't pursue the question further, but I wondered if it were that simple—one person, one past life, one future life? It didn't seem to me that my soul, intact at the time of death, simply returned again as me, but in another body. I recalled my early studies of the Seth materials, channeled by Jane Roberts. Seth explained the concept of the oversoul and maintained that the oversoul can actually exist in seven planes of existence at the same time. So, it seemed plausible that one great soul could exist in several human bodies at a time. I had to find a way to make sense of this for myself, but also to help my clients—some of whom struggled with the information—especially the many women who felt they *were* Mary Magdalene.

It would be a few years before I would finally find the language which made sense of it for me. My friend Merryl Sloane told me about a lovely evening she had spent in Tucson in the presence of an Indian woman, Sri Karunamayi, "who gave us the Divine Mother's blessings." Her eyes misted up as she recalled the feeling of looking into the woman's eyes. "She called us her Tucson babies. It was very sweet. She's an incarnation of the Divine Mother."

"What?" I asked. "She's the reincarnation of who?"

"No, not *the* reincarnation, *an* incarnation of the Divine Mother."

"That's it! That is the concept I've been searching for," I said. "She is a part of ... a manifestation of ... an energy. That explains what's going on with the numerous people reporting being the same person in a past life. They are *an* incarnation. We have been using the term 'reincarnation' as if describing a singular corporeal experience, when it is an immense and complex spiritual one."

My current thinking is that three different experiences may come up during a past-life regression. A person may indeed be recalling and reporting a past life; there are enough cases that have been validated through research to satisfy me that this can be the case. There are times when my clients and I feel that the material is more metaphorical, more like a dream, and is useful in helping them work through current life problems. The third type of experience is as an aspect of a larger spirit—an archetype, as I've discussed previously—one manifestation with the potential for many other manifestations of something greater: Divine Mother, Prophet, or Priestess.

Ruth Montgomery died in 2001, a little more than three years after we had met in Naples for the first time. I'm grateful for having known her and for the time we did spend together. She was a woman of tremendous courage to write so personally of things that are considered by many to be part of a lunatic fringe. She risked her solid reputation as a journalist as well as her livelihood. She can easily be credited with giving millions of people their first exposure to metaphysical concepts which are quite commonplace today. In her book *A World Beyond* (Fawcett Books, 1985), she wrote: "There are many rooms in the Father's House just as there are many grades in school. The period of time we spend on earth is but one grade of life. It is but a beginning." I got the impression from Sarah that Ruth planned to communicate with her earthly friends. I look forward to learning what she will teach us from the other side. I would love to know what she thinks of my theories.

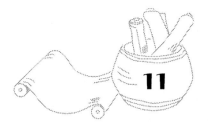

MARTHA AND THE FAMILY
IN BETHANY

*L*ily and I met at Ruth Montgomery's birthday celebration. I felt an immediate affinity for her. She was born and raised in France, of medium height, with a strong but slight body, one of those stunning women who, while still having a youthful face, has a head of brilliant white hair. Lily is a therapist who also, in her words, "works frequently with the invisible ones." She told me she felt she had known Jesus in a past life and might have been Martha. I was interested in learning more about Martha and was pleased that Lily agreed to a regression.

I knew from reading Ruth Montgomery's book and from working with other clients that Martha was part of that group of women who provided essential support to Jesus and his disciples as they traveled. Although the youngest in her family, she was the one concerned with keeping the household running smoothly. People referred to her as organized, dependable, serious. It also appears she would get frustrated that Mary Magdalene wouldn't help her, and envious when Mary took the time to join the men in discussion and travel.

As Lily/Martha relaxed into her regression session, she told me that her brother, Lazarus, who had never been a strong man, fell ill. Very ill. Everyone was worried that he would not survive, and they sent for Jesus (she preferred this version of his name), hoping that he might use his healing powers to help his friend. At the very least, they were sure he would want to say goodbye. Days passed and Jesus did not come. Lazarus fell into a deep sleep, and then he was gone. The family prepared his body and placed him in the family tomb. A few days after the burial, Jesus finally appeared. Martha was heartbroken and very, very angry.

"I'm mad at Jesus. He came too late. Mary [Magdalene] is here too and she feels the same as I. Jesus tries to console us in a tender and loving way. He puts his hand on my head. Whatever he says, I kind of understand. It soothes me a bit."

"What happens next?"

"Jesus asks to be led to Lazarus' tomb. He walks up to the opening and begins to pray. Mary and I stay close by. Jesus calls out Lazarus' name. Everybody hears his strong voice. 'Lazarus, come forth.'" She began to sob. "And I see Lazarus come out of the tomb. He is still in rags and wrappings. Jesus knew it would happen. He knew not to come earlier. He had received guidance to wait. He was told not to worry and to not interfere; it was not time. Then finally he heard that it was time to go see Lazarus. There was a plan. My love and respect for Lazarus grew immensely [because he had agreed at soul level to play this part]. It was time for me to learn. Life took on a different meaning. This miracle was so big, so incredible; life is not the same after something like that. One's vision gets bigger. Your little life, taking care of the house, people, worries—all gone. I feel blessed and privileged. I stepped to another level. I know now that I sit with a master."

"What was it like for your family after that?"

"It wasn't easy. Those who wished to discredit Jesus wanted to kill Lazarus. His life was in danger. They didn't want him to tell his story. We became more careful than we were naturally. However, it was in perspective, too. What more can happen? Death, resurrection—you know you are under the umbrella of God."

"How was your life changed after that?"

"I was most happy that my relationship with my sister Mary changed. We got close; we healed everything. She was so sweet. She forgave me for the way I had looked at her before and the way I had judged her."

After coming out of hypnosis, Lily and I talked about what she had recalled as Martha. We loved Martha's insight, "One's vision gets bigger. Your little life, taking care of the house, people, worries—all gone." Lily said, "My emotions were related to 'now I see what I didn't see before.' When the Holy Spirit came into me four years ago, I started helping people see that we can't know everything—like how upset Martha was that Jesus hadn't come.

"Nowadays, I am able to respond to a problem with 'I know this looks horrible, but it is because I don't know everything. There has to be a reason; it will be fine.' I now don't have to know everything, because I know it will turn out. Martha could have said, 'Jesus knows what he is doing; we don't have to be upset about this.' When I am in the energy of doing God's work, life is much easier. When you see the bigger picture from your spiritual eyes without questioning, you know there is much work being done in the invisible."

What Martha had reported was consistent with the past-life report of Ruth Montgomery's physician. I had regressed him just days earlier to a past life of having been that very brother, Lazarus. Ruth wrote of this session in her last book, *The World to Come* (Harmony Books, 1999), which she said she'd rather begrudgingly decided to finish—albeit with a twinkle in her eye—after my visit to Naples. Dr. Joseph Spano's rich and beautiful story is told in detail in chapter thirteen of her book, but I wanted to include a small excerpt from that session to demonstrate the consistency between his report and Lily's (Martha).

Lazarus described his illness and how he became weaker and weaker until finally his spirit separated and

[is] merging with something independent, yet with something larger. ... My sisters are crying and wailing. They don't want to

believe that I am dead. Martha is upset because she thought Jesus would intervene, but as I see it now, I can understand at a much deeper level that it was very important for him to wait for me to die.[12]

He also reported what Martha had stated: that there were those who wanted to kill him to discredit Jesus. He said,

[P]eople are telling me that the Pharisees want to see me dead because they realize the importance of Christ raising someone up from the dead, and they would like to have me dead again right away, to extinguish that.[13]

Lazarus avoided going to Jerusalem after that because "They are waiting for me."

After Martha realized that Jesus was indeed the Christ, Martha said, "I'm now going to join the others, traveling and teaching."

Aha, I thought. *Traveling and teaching.* Like Paul had observed, it appeared the women did have equal positions to the men in the beginning. Another piece of the puzzle of the Sisterhood fell into place.

---

12. Ruth Montgomery, *The World to Come* (New York: Harmony Books, 1999), p. 140.
13. Ibid, p. 143.

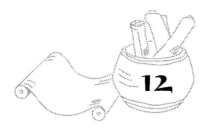

SARAH OF ARIMATHEA

*R*uth's dear friend, who I called Sarah (her name from her past life), did two sessions with me while I was in Naples. Sarah was close to Lazarus and his three sisters, as well as to Jeshua and his family. She spoke respectfully of her family and of the value they placed on education, even for the girls, and how several families (those of Zachariah, the father of John the Baptist; Joseph, the father of Jeshua; and hers, the daughter of Joseph of Arimathea) did Seder together.

"Today we are outside playing [smiling]. We are going to play hide and seek. We are running off to hide, and me and Jeshua and John start talking about God. We talk a lot about God in our homes, more than in other homes, I believe. When Father gives thanks, it is not just the ritual; it has meaning."

Curious because I had my own past-life picture of John the Baptist, I asked, "So you play with John? Will you tell me about John?"

"He has a full head of curly hair, light skin; personality, kind of rough—not polished. Even though he is from here, he is different from other children. John's a little mischievous and likes action—very vocal. That's partly ego. I feel he likes to get attention that way. I'd call him a rebel—if we go one way, he'll go the other. He's like that even with his parents. He's not exactly a black sheep ... just different."

"Very interesting. Thank you. And what is Jeshua like?"

"Jeshua is beautiful; he has elegant fingers. He is radiant even as a boy [about twelve now]. John is dense, tougher, sturdier. There is an awareness among the families of a need to protect Jeshua. My father is touched by seeing him. He respects Jeshua. We already know that he's not one of us."

She broke into a huge smile and her present-life persona began speaking. "I see white light and I hear the voice of Jeshua. He says, 'Yes, you did know me. I am all that ever was and all that will ever be. I'm here to help you.' It's happening ... I'm feeling the expansiveness and seeing the light, and it is brilliant. He says that the only thing between me and him is doubt. He is telling me that I'm a pure soul, unique. Through the ages I've managed to stay connected to the light and not the blemishes."

I understood what Jeshua was talking about. I experienced Sarah's purity and uniqueness as she watched after Ruth Montgomery, as she shepherded me around Naples, and as she cared for her family. She radiates love. Her greatest challenge, we learned, is to remember to take time for herself.

A few days later, we met for a second regression. This time, she told me about how she and many other women had taught right alongside the men. The following dialogue occurred near the end of the session. It had been several years since Jeshua's death, and she was speaking to a group of people.

"I hold my chin high and move to the foreground. I'm well educated and strong. I am emancipated. The chains [of the culture] are off. I address men, women, and children, traveling and spreading the word."

"Please tell me more about your travels."

"My father owns a fleet of ships, and the apostles and I travel on his ships. I know Paul; he sometimes travels with us. I help organize the foreign travels. I myself went to England. I did not marry so that I could spread the word, and I did so for almost twenty years. I wrote about our work at home and abroad." She paused with a puzzled look on her face. "What happened to that [written material]?"

"Please move into the future and see if you can discover what became of your writings."

"I see they have been put aside. I'm feeling anger and bitterness and outrage! I am an equal. I can match these men. I'm angry at these fishermen who aren't as educated as I. I'm sensing the women's anger towards Paul. When he took women out of the movement, the balance was destroyed. That didn't happen with Jeshua. He held women in high esteem."

"Please move forward now to the end of your Sarah lifetime."

"After more than twenty years, I returned to Jerusalem to help care for my family. The Romans are destroying Solomon's Temple. Everything is falling apart. The movement left Jerusalem for Rome. People who didn't even know Jeshua are taking it and moving it to their political arena in order to control people. They moved north. It is in the men's hands now; the women are the healers, but the Romans are patriarchal. Women exist to be beautiful. The Good News now must fit into their patriarchal paradigm. I die angry!"

"Please now move forward into your present life and see things from your wise-self perspective."

"Yes. The women have to set things straight now [in the twenty-first century]. The movement got out of balance and it set us back. Now we women have to pick it up again. [Laughing] I see my grandmother from this lifetime. She is waving a flag and saying, 'Go for it, girl!'"

After this session, Sarah and I enjoyed lunch in her beautiful backyard with its lush, tropical landscaping. Like many Naples residents who take advantage of the numerous inlets and bays there, her family has a boat dock adjacent to their yard. They are often blessed with personal visits from a friendly manatee, one of the strangest sea mammals I've ever seen. We talked about the number of people within her circle of friends and acquaintances who were reporting being reincarnated Essenes. Ruth Montgomery was the catalyst for it all. I was excited about my session with her later that afternoon.

Ruth already had a great deal of information regarding her past life as another Ruth, sister of Lazarus, Mary, and Martha, through previous hypnoregression work and automatic writing. She was hoping to learn something new today. After she was in trance, I prompted her to enter her past life during a happy time with her family. She spoke of the time her and Jeshua's families lived together in Egypt after fleeing from Herod's threat to kill infant boys. Lazarus and Jeshua were very close in age. Ruth reported that she was seven years old when the boys were born, and she was about fourteen or fifteen when they returned home from the Alexandria region—her family going to Bethany, and Joseph and Mary's to Nazareth. I prompted her to move forward.

"Mother has died, and I now have taken over the care of the family. I don't mind."

"Tell me about your siblings, Ruth," I suggested.

"Lazarus is a scholar. Father thought he might follow in his footsteps and become a rabbi, but while he likes his studies, I don't think he wants to become a priest. Martha helps me out with household chores and is a hard worker. Mary helps too, but she's a dreamer." She sighed and looked melancholy.

"What are you remembering, Ruth?"

"I'm to be married soon."

"You don't seem very happy about it."

"It's an appropriate match, which father approves of, but Jonathan is an old and sober man. I would rather spend more time at the monastery myself, but I don't have any choice in the matter."

After her marriage, Ruth lived in another city but visited her family when she could. As she had children of her own, there was little time for reading or studies.

"I'm remembering our time in Egypt and some of the mysteries to which we were exposed. Jeshua and Lazarus and I speak of them from time to time. I miss that. There's a group forming around Jeshua now; they study together and travel. I want to go with them."

"Do you find a way to do that?"

"I beg Jonathan to allow me to go with them. Not full time. Just once in a while."

"Does he know who Jeshua is—what he means to you?"

"He knows him, yes, but he doesn't think he's the Anointed One at all. He thinks he's a heretic who speaks against the teachings of the rabbis. He forbids me to go."

"Do you find a way to make peace with this?"

"I stop asking, but I still long to be with them— [with] Jeshua, my family. One day I leave my children in the charge of our servants and take off in search of them. I need this!"

"Do you catch up with the group?"

"Oh, yes." She smiled and appeared to be relaxed for the first time during this session. "Yes, I see Jeshua teaching. I spend the day there listening to him and talking to my sisters. Afterwards, I tell Jeshua I want to go with him. But he says I need to return home and care for my children. He says that the role of mother is very important and that I should teach my children what he teaches others."

"Did that time with him help you?"

"Yes." She sighed. "I do return home." She looked stricken. "Jonathan was furious because I went against his wishes. I'm held prisoner in my own home after that."

Ruth Montgomery was silent for quite a while. I was about to ask her to move forward again when she said, "Julia, these are all things I know already. I was hoping to learn something new today."

It is often the case that those who have a lot of information about a past life—whether it is from reading historical accounts, having psychic readings, or (in Ruth's case) channeling the information through automatic writing—will repeat what they know, not unlike how a story becomes solid through repeated retellings. But Ruth wanted more, so I prompted her high self to recall something about which her current mind knew nothing. She sank back into her pillows and took a deep breath.

"I'm at the monastery working with Judith today. I'm learning to read the Akashic records."

"What is the process?"

"I close my eyes, empty my mind and focus on a person—drink in their essence, so to speak. I first see their physical features, then I look beyond the physical. The first time I saw someone's soul history—just their previous lifetime—I was so excited. After a while I was able to think of a person and go directly to their whole soul history."

"No wonder being cut off from Jeshua and your siblings was so painful for you."

"It was."

"It appears you have that same ability today, in your Ruth Montgomery incarnation."

She smiled. Ruth was an exceptionally modest woman. She had brushed aside the praise we women heaped upon her at her birthday party a few days earlier. I felt that same modesty in her past-life persona because she did not report the extent of her abilities. Her friend Dr. Spano, speaking as Lazarus, did, however.

He said, "Ruth was very smart, very bright, quite intelligent. ... I hear that she is very well-versed in the ancient mysteries. One might call her somewhat of a priestess. It is something to do with temples of Egypt, maybe something with Isis. It was an ancient teaching, something Ruth would have had in common with Jesus. She may even have taught him."[14]

I looked over the notes from my first week in Naples. I had heard reports from intelligent, gifted women who had been deeply involved in the evolution of consciousness two thousand years ago, who had become frustrated. Sarah's written accounts were nowhere to be found. Ruth's education and gifts during that time were suppressed, as she was literally placed under house arrest. I reflected that these women and men here in southern Florida must derive great joy from being together at this time—out in the open with their beliefs, and using their gifts without fear.

---

14. Ruth Montgomery, *The World to Come*, pp. 134-135.

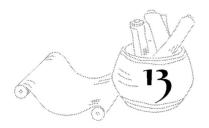

MAGPIE: A WOMAN OF VALUE

*S*arah had insisted that Jeshua held women in high esteem. My understanding of how deeply Jeshua valued women, as well as how he and they worked with energy, broadened during my work with a businesswoman from Oregon. Tall and slender with long blonde hair, she was in her early forties when we met. In spite of her stunning beauty, she seemed curiously indifferent to it. However, her dedication to creating beautiful environments through her interior decorating business offset this indifference. Educated in Catholic schools, she insisted even as a child that she "knew" what Jesus would say about certain things. She wanted to undergo past-life regression to confirm for herself what an adept had told her in a reading: that she had known Jeshua "on another plane."

I learned that her name during that incarnation was Maggie. Jeshua, who often referred to people by affectionate nicknames, called her Magpie (of course, all past-life names are translated through the English-speaking minds of my clients). She had met

Jeshua on several occasions over the years, and she was eighteen at the time of the following meeting.

"He is staying with some people I know, and I am invited to dinner. I have a hundred questions to ask. I let the men talk most of the time. The only other woman there is the wife of the host, and she is serving the food. I know their son; he's a show-off. He has a sword on. His mother told him to go change."

I prompted her to go to a significant event.

"After dinner we [Jeshua and she] go into the garden. I ask Jeshua, 'Why am I so different?' 'Because you were born partially awake,' he answers. I ask him why I was born a woman and therefore cannot follow him [as he travels]. He answers, 'The energies of the woman are important. They balance the planet. You are to walk the earth with compassion and freedom of spirit, and others will feel it.' He explains that I am an equal to men. I am important."

I said, "The energies of the woman balance the planet and are *equal* to men. Powerful words. Please go on."

"Yes. I am sitting on a bench without my sandals on. He touches my feet. I cross them because I'm embarrassed." She bit her lip and did look embarrassed. "He takes water from the fountain and puts it on my feet. He says, 'You are the water, you are the sky. You are the arms of the tree.'" Hearing this, she began to weep. Tears rolled down my own cheeks as well. "He doesn't want me to be anxious any more."

"What is the meaning of Jeshua washing your feet?"

"Washing of feet is done to an honored guest."

"So Jeshua is telling you that you are an honored guest. Also that your energy is important and balances male energy. Do you believe him?"

"Yes—a part of me says yes, but a part says I shouldn't say yes."

Her mother had taught her that a woman's role is to serve men, and to consider herself an equal flew in the face of deep tradition. In a subsequent session I learned of her progress towards acceptance of her value. Several years had passed, and Magpie and Jeshua had become intimate friends.

"We are sitting on a bench. I have great power now. Because of his high calling, I agreed not to interfere [by pressing for more from him]. I tease him that I am so spoiled by him that I will never marry. But I will assist with the work."

"Are you in love with him?"

"Yes. [She blushes] I'm touching and holding his face, and he is holding my arms." She demonstrated how they would sit opposite each other and touch hands, exchanging energy. "I sometimes get confused when he teaches me about energy. If I keep the energy running in my heart, I won't get confused. If the energy runs wild, it gets mixed up with sexual desire, so I'm trying to run it through the heart."

This woman expressed certainty about her past-life relationship with Jeshua, including the energy exchange. It seemed to be interfering with her present-life relationships. "Who can measure up to him?" she asked.

I would hear that over and over again as I met more and more women with reports of past lives of having known Jeshua. Like this woman, many of them are single and enjoy rich and meaningful lives. And in all relationships, they demand nothing less than equality.

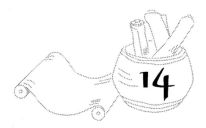

SHANNON AND THE 444S

*T*rue to their word, my guides saw to it that I knew where I would be going after leaving Ruth Montgomery's community of friends. When I learned that the great Buddhist teacher Thich Nhat Hahn would be in Key West during the first part of November, conducting a week-long retreat sponsored by the Omega Institute, I knew I needed to be there. I called Omega and was gratified to learn I could still register. The drive from Florida's west coast proved lovely but uneventful in spite of roadside warnings to watch for alligators crossing the road. I later learned this highway is called Alligator Alley. Heading to the southernmost part of the continental United States, crossing island after palm tree–covered island, left me exhilarated.

While I thoroughly enjoyed the experience of being in silence with hundreds of people, hearing Thich Nhat Hahn lecture in person, and being charmed by the beauty of the nuns and monks who accompanied him, on the evening of the second day I learned why I had been guided to Key West. As I was walking to supper, I felt a tug on my left sleeve and turned to see who it was. A blonde woman beamed at me, holding out a copy of *The Messengers.* Startled and utterly confused, I wondered how she knew who I was—we didn't wear name badges and we held no conversations. I was certain I had never seen her before. Hastily, I opened the little notepad we'd been given and wrote, "Who are you, and what are you doing with my book?" She wrote back, "Will you break the silence after dinner so we can talk?" I smiled and nodded yes.

Shannon Anderson introduced herself as a therapist from northern Florida. We discovered that we'd called Omega the same day to see if there were last-minute openings for this retreat. She said, "I didn't know why, but I knew I had to come to this." She explained that she had been having 444 experiences for many years and was thrilled and validated to read about Nick's own 444 experiences and those of his friends. "I know that God's angels are behind this."

"I agree they are, but," I asked, "how did you know who I was?" She explained that she was at Key West Airport picking up a friend who had flown in for the retreat. As she was loading her friend's luggage into the trunk, a woman approached, asking if they were part of the Thich Nhat Hahn retreat. Shannon answered yes, and the woman, who I'll call Leisle, hopped into the back seat of her car. Amused and realizing that the woman thought she must be some shuttle service from Omega, Shannon slung Leisle's suitcase into the trunk beside her friend's.

On the drive to the resort where the retreat was being held, the three women talked. Shannon asked if they believed in angels and told them about some of her 444 experiences. Leisle, a German-born tour director living in London and a long-time Buddhist, incorrectly explained that Buddhists do not believe in angels. (Some sects of Buddhism do.) Shannon dropped the subject.

When I moved into my assigned condo, my roommates were a woman from Manhattan and Leisle from London. Leisle and I got acquainted during the evening before the retreat started. Since I had been working on *The Lost Sisterhood*, I shared a little about my work, my call to hit the road, and how grateful I was that my first book had provided me with sufficient income to take a year off.

She admired the angel on the cover of *The Messengers*, but didn't say much more. I was not aware of her conversation with Shannon about angels earlier in the day. Nor did I know, until Shannon told me the rest of the story, that the following evening Leisle got together with Shannon and saw her copy of *The Messengers* sitting on the table. Leisle remarked, "Oh, you are reading this? The author is my roommate." Shannon was beside herself and said she couldn't wait to find me. I know it was no accident that we were walking to dinner at the same moment so that she would find me. I think she got a kick out of surprising me the way she did.

During our after-dinner conversation, she told me about her training and practice in past-life regression and mentioned that she had worked with a woman who reported a lifetime as Mary Magdalene. I grinned. "I think I need to meet her, Shannon."

"Well, good," she said. "I think that can be arranged, and I would love it if you would come and speak to our *Course in Miracles* group next week." I replied that my guides had told me to say yes to invitations like hers.

I stayed over a few days in Key West before I headed north to Shannon's home near St. Augustine. I underestimated how long the drive would take and arrived at the meeting hall a few minutes after the group had assembled. The moment I sat down, Shannon turned the evening over to me. That was trust! I talked for about fifteen or twenty minutes and then opened it up to questions. A lively discussion ensued and the time went by quickly. I was very tired from my long day on the road, but since I needed to follow Shannon to the place she'd arranged for me to sleep, I stayed for the after-meeting refreshments and socializing. While I signed a few books and listened to some personal stories, I noticed a young man standing a few feet back from the group. I'd noticed him earlier because he had said nothing during the discussion, smiling sweetly throughout. Finally, as the group thinned, and the food was put away, he walked up to me. He said, "It is so good to see you again, Sister." I didn't remember ever meeting him, but that didn't mean I hadn't, so I thanked him and said it was good to see him, too. Then he hugged me, stepped back, looked at me with beautiful sea-green eyes, said, "Feed my sheep," turned, and walked out of the building.

As Shannon and I walked outside to our cars, I said, "I just got a hug from someone who I think believes he's Jesus." Shannon laughed and said, "Oh, you met him? Yes, he does. He's very sweet, and hasn't been a problem. So. what did you think?"

Since she is also a therapist, we talked about how we each handle situations like this. He wasn't a client, but she had encountered situations such as I had, where clients lacked the ego strength to appropriately process material that spontaneously came up or was reported under hypnosis. We agreed that some people aren't appropriate for regression work. Others needed assistance in interpreting the material, making it useful to them, and *not* overidentifying with whom they had been or whom they thought they had been in a past life.

I thought back to a couple of these experiences. The first was in the 1970s when I had worked in a psychiatric hospital, very early in my career as a therapist and before I knew anything about past lives. One of our patients believed she was Mary—a pregnant Mary, preparing to give birth to Jesus. She was not pregnant but she looked it, and in her confused mind she was convinced of her story. I've since wondered how I might work with her today, and whether she could successfully integrate the archetype of Mary into her psyche. She had been given Thorazine, an antipsychotic medication, and within a few days the delusion had disappeared. Hypnosis and regression therapy are contraindicated for anyone who is delusional anyway, so I would only have been able to work with her once she stepped back into reality. Like the man from Shannon's group, Mary was very sweet and frequently bestowed blessings upon staff and patients alike.

The second experience, which happened after *The Messengers* came out, was disturbing. A man drove a considerable distance to have a session with me. He stated that he was a reincarnated apostle and wanted to know more about his mission in this life. That was fine; I frequently hear things like that. However, as I led him through my usual hypnotic induction process, rather than reporting memories from a present or past life, his voice deepened and he spoke in a very stern manner. I thought he was probably channeling. He identified himself as one of the righteous, and one who was entitled to the priesthood by inheritance. There was much fire-and-brimstone pontificating, and finally he spoke directly to me. He berated me, calling me arrogant, and then delivered some "orders." Because this was unexpected, I was taken aback but also very annoyed. I brought him out of the trance and asked him to sit up and take a big drink of water. I then asked him if he remembered what he'd just said. He replied that he had, and that he'd been sent by the Brotherhood to set me straight. I handed his money back and said, "You certainly have a right to your beliefs, but you have no right to come here and challenge mine." I stood up and walked out of the room. It wasn't my responsibility—or even my right professionally—to argue with his beliefs or ethics. My only regret was giving his money back. "Yes," said Shannon later. "We deal with all kinds of clients, don't we?"

Looking forward to meeting Shannon's client the following day, but exhausted from my very long drive, I fell into a deep, dreamless sleep that night. As this was my first trip to the South, I was grateful that, the following morning, Shannon took the time to show me some historical sights, including a drive through beautiful St. Augustine, the nation's oldest city. There are enough preserved buildings that I really got the feeling of what life in this city might have been like when the Spanish first explored and then occupied the New World. I would like to spend more time there someday. As we wound through the countryside, Shannon and I talked more about her own experiences. She said she was extremely interested in the Grail stories and that research and myth were pointing her to southern France and to the many Magdalene cults there. I told her I'd read some of the books about which she was excited, including Michael Baigent's *Holy Blood, Holy Grail* (Dell, 1983), and two of Margaret Starbird's books *The Woman with the Alabaster Jar* (Bear & Company, 1993) and *The Goddess in the Gospels* (Bear & Company, 1998). I asked her if she had worked with anyone in past-life regression who reported knowledge of Mary Magdalene being in France. She said that her information—her belief in this theory—came more from research and her own "knowing."

Shannon has kept in touch with me over the years since we first met. She has made numerous trips to the historic sites of the Cathars and the Knights Templar, as well as to many churches in southern France where Saint Mary Magdalene is revered. She's writing a book on her remarkable experiences (packed with synchronistic events), which I'm looking forward to reading.

When we arrived for our appointment that evening with Shannon's client, a physician, the woman's husband offered to take their small children and Shannon for a car ride so we could work together without interruption. We agreed on ninety minutes for our session. She was an excellent hypnosis subject and did report being Mary Magdalene.

Excerpts of her session appear in later parts of the book, but I'll include here the most startling excerpt, which occurred close to the end of her session. "Jeshua says, 'Ma nish-ta-naw ha-lai-law ha-zeh. Blasphemy! You say the words as if they have meaning, but you don't understand what they mean. Why is this night different than all others?'"

"What does he mean, Mary?"

"He means [it is time to] let go of the ritual that holds on to past grievances. It is time to forgive. To teach a ritual that holds on to anger, blame, and pain is in fact a blasphemy."

Her power was appreciable and very aligned with other women I was meeting during my cross-country journey. This particular incarnation of Mary was adamant that among their goals—hers, Jeshua's, and the men and women involved in the movement—was to help their fellow Jews move beyond repeating old stories that encouraged hanging on to past grievances. Jeshua went beyond encouraging people to forgive their ancient enemies, however. According to Mary, he said it was a blasphemy not to do so. Furthermore, she claimed Jeshua wanted people to stop rote memorization and to become leaders. Shannon's client clarified that Jeshua wanted all people to think for themselves and to stop blindly following the priests with their old rituals. No wonder he was such a threat to their authority.

I remembered what Suddee had said about rituals at the Mount Carmel Monastery. "I did away with many of the old rules and rituals of my fathers, because the purpose behind them had been forgotten and so distorted that they now were meaningless. ... We taught no meaningless ritual in my school."

Amazing, I thought. *Here's confirmation that something Suddee had taught a hundred years earlier, Jeshua had later attempted to instill in his followers.* That night, I gave thanks to the spirit guides and angels who had engineered the mystical meeting between me and Shannon, so that I could record what I heard that evening.

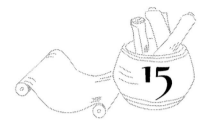

THE TWIN FLAME OF CHRIST

*I*n the past decade or two there have been many books and articles written about "the Magdalene."[15] These accounts range from scholarly (*The Woman Jesus Loved: Mary Magdalene in the Nag Hammadi Library* [Antti Marjanen, Brill Academic Pub., 1996] and *The Woman with the Alabaster Jar* [Margaret Starbird, Bear & Company, 1993]) to channeled (*I Remember Union: The Story of Mary Magdalena* [Flo Calhoun, Jayn Zopf, and Hannah Kleber, All Worlds Pub., 1992]) to religious fiction (*The Magdalene Gospel: What If Women Had Written the Gospels?* [Mary Ellen Ashcroft, Doubleday, 1995]). Then there's the enormous success of *The Da Vinci Code* (Dan Brown, Doubleday, 2003), a thriller with the core thesis that not only were Mary and Jesus married but they had at least one child and hence, the Holy Grail is actually the womb of Mary Magdalene.

---

15. Why was Mary of Bethany called Magdalen or Magdalene? Margaret Starbird, author of *The Woman with the Alabaster Jar*, presents a theory that the name refers to the Magdal-eder, or watchtower of the flock—the stronghold of the Daughter of Zion referred to in the *Book of Micah* in the Old Testament. Starbird says, "It would have been the Hebrew equivalent of calling her 'Mary the Great.'" The more commonly held belief is that her family originally came from a town called Magdala.

Why the sudden renewal of interest in this woman? Who was she really? Some believe she was rescued by a compassionate Jesus from prostitution and then became one of his disciples (although, in the late 1960s, the Catholic Church acknowledged that that story was not about Mary Magdalene at all, but about another woman). Paul (through the memory of Nick Bunick as related in *The Messengers*) reported that Mary Magdalene was a member of the family of Lazarus with whom Jesus stayed when in Bethany. Many others believe that Mary Magdalene was Jesus' companion, lover, and even his wife.

Through research and the revelations of regression subjects, I have come to believe that Mary Magdalene was the twin flame, the feminine counterpart, to Jesus. Twin flames are souls who are partners with a mission which extends beyond one lifetime, usually to several lifetimes. Jesus needed Mary's feminine energy to complement his masculine energy. Because of the unbalanced domination of masculine energy during her lifetime and beyond, she has not been given credit for her considerable role. But, as we continue to explore the various Magdalene stories which have been brought to me, you may come to believe that Mary Magdalene was not only Jesus' companion, but a major teacher and healer in her own right.

The Gospel of Philip is one of the fifty-two papyrus books found near the town of Nag Hammadi in Egypt in 1945. Also called the Gnostic Gospels, these are the sacred texts of one of the earliest of the Christian sects, hidden for almost a millennium and a half in the dry dust of a secret cave. Researchers cannot say for certain when these books and papyrus sheets were written, but some may have been written about the same time as the Gospels of Matthew, Mark, Luke and John, or even earlier. Now called the Nag Hammadi Library, some of these texts state that they are a record of "the living Jesus" and offer to reveal "the mysteries" which Jesus taught to his disciples.

The companion of the Savior is Mary Magdalene. But Christ loved her more than all the disciples, and used to kiss her often on her mouth. The rest of the disciples were offended. ... They asked him, "Why do you love her more than all of us?" Jeshua answered and said to them, "Why do I not love you as I love her?"[16]

The answer to this question will become obvious as we continue to examine what a combination of information from the Gnostic Gospels and my clients' regression sessions have revealed. Together, they give us a composite picture of Mary Magdalene's full life.

She lived with her family in Bethany, a short walk from Jerusalem. They were part of an extended family or community, which included Joseph and Myrium and their children. There was an older sister, Ruth, then Lazarus, Mary, and finally Martha. Parents were seldom mentioned in any of the regression sessions, and it appears that even though Martha was the youngest, she took on the role of mother, while Lazarus seemed to be a father figure to his sisters. Even in her teens, Mary Magdalene preferred to spend her time with the men discussing spiritual matters.

Lazarus and Jeshua were about the same age, Mary just a little younger—perhaps only a year or two, probably no more than four. The two families got together from time to time, and Mary and Jeshua apparently knew each other from childhood.

Sarah of Arimathea (as reported by Ruth Montgomery's friend) described Mary Magdalene as strong in personality but usually quiet. "She is slender, slight of build, with graceful hands. Her hair is long and dark and full. Mary is always connected to Spirit and often seems to be in her own world. When she is in the company of Jeshua, she blossoms like a flower. She laughs more when he is around and is rather melancholy when he is away. She is very much in love with him. But it is more. Jeshua is the only man who understands her. He acknowledges her, as he acknowledges Woman: the Giver of Life, the Creator.

"Among the other women, Mary Magdalene is held in high esteem. There is a group of mystical women who meet underground,

---

16. *The Gospel of Philip* (Saying 138), The Nag Hammadi Library (NHL)

in private, in a secluded place. She seems to be the leader. She is the counterpart of Jeshua. She can tap into knowledge."

"What do you mean?" I asked.

"Someone will ask a question she hasn't thought about before, and the answer comes to her. She can tap into Divine Source," Sarah said.

In *The Dialogue of the Savior* (Saying 235) from the Nag Hammadi Library, Mary Magdalene is praised as a visionary and as "one who knows the All."

Ruth, Jeshua's sister (as reported by Carol), said, "Jeshua needed the union between him and Mary Magdalene in order to complete his mission. It was through the blending of their energies that he was able to come into perfect balance and to work with energy in such a way that he appeared to perform miracles. When one is in balance, it is then possible to move into other dimensions in order to strengthen the connection to the Source of all love."

Later, Ruth said, "Mary Magdalene performed initiations for women and men." This is consistent with the belief that Mary Magdalene was a sacred woman or temple priestess. Margaret Starbird wrote in *The Woman with the Alabaster Jar*:

> The anointing performed by the woman at Bethany was similar to the familiar ritual practice of a sacred priestess ... in the Goddess cults of the Roman Empire. ... In the ancient world, sexuality was considered sacred, a special gift from the goddess of love, and the priestesses who officiated at the temples ... were considered holy ... "consecrated women" ... At some periods of Jewish history, they were even a part of the ritual worship in the Temple of Jerusalem.[17]

Another Oregon woman, through her memory of also having been Jeshua's sister, Ruth, spoke of her love for Mary Magdalene. "I was in awe. Just absolute awe. I thought Mary Magdalene was perfect. She was older and more experienced than I was."

---

17. Starbird, *The Woman with the Alabaster Jar* (Santa Fe: Bear & Company, 1993), p. 29.

Mary had given Ruth some bracelets. In retelling the story, this woman said, "Right after I remembered that, I bought this bracelet [holding out her arm for me to see] and I haven't taken it off since. Actually, Mary gave me three bracelets; one was gold. I still get chills now talking about it. One was silver and another copper. Mary told me they would bring me prosperity, spiritual balance, and physical health. I cherished them and carried them with me my whole life." With a laugh, she added, "I wish I knew where they were today."

My clients described Mary as a priestess, a wise teacher, a good friend, a perfect woman. They also spoke of her as Jeshua's companion, spiritual counterpart, and wife. Clearly, she represents the archetypes of Divine Feminine and Sacred Helpmate.

The first client to report the wedding of Mary and Jeshua was little Ruth.

"I'm very excited," reported little Ruth. "I have a part to play in the ceremony. I am to give them the cup. The room is beautiful. Lots of lamps and so much food. Mother is crying."

"It sounds like you are getting ready for a celebration. What is it?"

"My brother is getting married."

"Which brother?"

"Jeshua," she stated with obvious pride. "And I am to have a part."

"And who is to be his bride?"

"Mary, of course." Her voice implied I should have known. She was referring to Mary Magdalene.

"Please move forward in time, to the ceremony."

"I have a special cloth around my neck. It is about four inches wide and a burgundy color. It goes around my neck and hangs down the front. I bring the cup they are to drink from. I walk up to them and hand them the cup. Jeshua and Mary take it together. Then I stand back. They face each other and hold the cup together. Then each one takes a drink. Then the officiate acknowledges the joining." The client explained later that the joining was both a declaration that they were now husband and wife and also the joining of their chakras, a joining of energies.

"The people behind me are holding hands in a circle all around."

In another session, I had asked Myrium to recall Jeshua's wedding day. Laughingly, she stated, "He turned water into wine. That's my boy!" Her mood quickly changed as she sighed dreamily. "They look so beautiful. It's evening, and we have lit fires. It's so beautiful."

"How is this wedding different from others?"

"There is a shower of light coming down on them. The presence of the angels. They were there. How can I explain? Every wedding is a blessed event. Every wedding lifts the couple from the vibrational frequency in which they reside to a higher level. With a high-frequency couple, there is much, much light present. This will carry them into a higher union. Ceremony honors connection and lifts them to a higher level—one they can support energetically. This union feels good in every way. The light is pulsating through. Everybody feels it. Oh, for goodness sakes! The glory of this couple!"

"Would you talk about little Ruth's part in the ceremony?"

"Yes, she's so cute. She felt very special. It was all about her, you know [smiles]. She's giving them the cup of love. That's why she's so important. And Jeshua plays that up. They can't be married without her, he says. [Laughing hard] She likes to be special, and he just pours it into her. She's so sweet and endearing, people want to pinch her cheeks."

Another client, a chiropractor from Washington state also reported Magdalene memories. To her, I said, "Some of the Mary Magdalene aspects say there was a physical marriage between her and Jeshua."

"Oh yes!"

"And some say it was spiritual only. You are saying yes to the physical marriage? Do you remember the marriage, the wedding?"

"Yes, there was a physical marriage and a spiritual one. The physical marriage was a union, a commitment to each other. The spiritual was about harmony—the honoring with great respect [of] the yin/yang or male/female in each other. The knowing of who one is kept foremost. I feel the oneness of Jeshua and Mary. It's kind of like being merged."

A woman from Southern California reported, "God is here; angels are here as we exchange vows. I say, 'forever ... I love you. We are as one.' I see us as one. He says, 'I am one with you.' We are energetically together. Every cell of our being melting together. ... our marriage is a complete union."

"How do things change after the union?" I asked.

"I know more ... words, thoughts, deeper, more profound."

Many clients have referred to the wedding of Jeshua and Mary Magdalene, and some, although not all, report they had children. "Children were very important for Jeshua and Mary. They loved their children greatly because they were created in the image and likeness of unconditional love," said one.

Another woman reported the birth of Mary's first child. "I'm with Myrium and I'm pregnant with our first. Jeshua is sweet, attentive, and loving. I'm walking now. I'm in labor. [My mother-in-law] is very excited. As we walk, Jeshua has one hand on my shoulder and one on my lower back. It takes the pressure away, so the contractions are not so strong. I'm staying in radiant light so I can be totally and completely focused ... allowing the body to do its work." She laughed. "Myrium is kinda bossy. She's directing him where to put his hands. She can be forceful. She is such a love, such a love." I could hear the tenderness and love she felt for Jeshua's mother in her voice. She began to weep. "My life wouldn't be what it is without her."

Another woman said she gave birth in a tent with her mother-in-law in attendance. Tears of joy covered her cheeks as she spoke. "I wanted a girl. I'm scared and I'm happy ... crying and laughing at this miracle of creation. I say to Myrium, 'Have you ever seen such a thing as this?' Thank you so much, God, for this miracle, this love, this life, this husband, this earth. So much is given! We name her Martha."

Myrium cared for Jeshua and Mary Magdalene's children when the couple traveled. She observed that Mary Magdalene felt conflicted about it, but her mother-in-law assured her that the children had "many mothers." Mary Magdalene knew her place was with Jeshua.

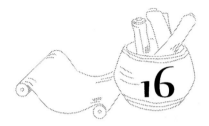

THE EROS OF SPIRITUALITY

Jeshua said to them,
"When you make the two into one,
when you make the inner like the outer
and the outer like the inner,
and the upper like the lower,
when you make male and female into
a single one,
so that the male will not be male
and the female will not be female ...
then you will enter the kingdom."[18]

While my clients were not in total agreement about the details of Jeshua's relationship with Mary Magdalene, the vast majority agreed they had an intimate and sexual relationship. I shared some of the material with a fellow writer. He was distressed. "I'm going to give you my first reaction. I feel repulsed to think of Jeshua as being sexual."

---

18. *The Gospel of Thomas* (Saying 22), NHL.

"You don't think he was fully human then, with human desires?" He thought about it. "This may be coming from a young place in me, maybe a place that needs all authority to be pure and perfect." This writer had done a lot of personal work, including psychotherapy and personal growth training. He was in touch with different inner voices, including what he refers to as his inner child. "And that young place believes sex is not pure or perfect, maybe even repulsive?" I asked.

His reaction was actually similar to my own at the beginning of this journey. It is what we have been taught. Far back in history, the religious authorities apparently couldn't bear to associate sex and God, and they got rid of the problem by creating the myth of the Virgin Mother and of the celibate, non-sexual Son of God. However, the very thing Jeshua and his group were trying to teach—according to my clients and recent scholarship—was that God was within each person. Jeshua said we were all like him, that we could do everything he did if we just woke up to who we are. To make Jeshua and his mother not human by denying their sexuality is the very antithesis of what he taught.

Through their explicit memories and visions, my clients showed me that Jeshua and his associates had incorporated Eastern beliefs about the sacredness of sexuality and about the necessity of utilizing sexual energy to achieve balance. My client Carol spoke several times of this sexual energy. I asked her to explain. "The primary purpose was to bring balance. But healing took place as a result. In your time, you call this energy by many names: kundalini, tantra, chi, but it is all the same. However, it was set up that the second chakra would run the most energy. It is the most powerful and easiest place to connect. It was not about sex. It was an unbelievable feeling of connecting, of being one with another person. The body experiences complete peace. It moves everything into balance. The goal was balance—androgyny."

The idea of androgyny—that is, of having one's masculine and feminine qualities in balance—is frequently found in the Gnostic Gospels. The excerpt from the *Gospel of Thomas* which opens this chapter is reflective of many such ancient references to the belief that to "enter the kingdom" one needs to achieve a balance, a blend, a marriage of the male and female qualities within oneself. Jewish mysticism is similarly replete with such references. Indigenous cultures worldwide also espouse the necessity of the balance of male/female to move into the mystic realm. In China it is referred to as balancing yin/yang. The Chinese yin/yang reference to masculine and feminine energy, rather than to male and female bodies, helps us to understand that it is *qualities* rather than *gender* which is being referenced.

Many of my women clients discovered that as they became more open to their own mystical nature, they were able to call upon the best of their masculine as well as their feminine qualities. Some of them also became aware that their erotic feelings towards others moved easily between yin and yang.

How, I wondered, would it be of value to people in my time to think that Jeshua was perhaps androgynous? A need *not to be female* runs very deep in many men and shows up clearly in past-life regression work. Pioneer past-life therapist Helen Wambaugh, Ph.D., accumulated data from hundreds of subjects participating in group regression sessions. Her results suggested that most souls have spent about half their incarnations as male and half as female. Apparently, in the safety of anonymous group sessions, the ego doesn't work so hard to select which genders will be "allowed" to be remembered. In one-on-one sessions in my office, women freely report both male and female lives, and report them in about the expected fifty-fifty ratio. Some express surprise at finding themselves in a man's body, but readily accept it. They will talk about their wives and sweethearts with ease. My male clients, on the other hand, report male lifetimes at the rate of about eighty to ninety percent. I seldom encounter men who regress to female past lives. And when I do, it is even rarer that they will refer to husbands and boyfriends without some discomfort.

I received a letter from a *Messengers* reader, telling me how grateful he was that the book had inspired him to get in touch with the meaning of his own past lives. He wrote that to know who he has been helped him to understand the totality of who he is now. I read through the synopsis of sixteen of his past lifetimes and discovered they were all male. Not only that, many were strong, aggressive figures. Where was the balance? I wrote back suggesting that if he were certain he wanted to understand the totality of who he is, he would need to investigate his lifetimes as a woman.

Jeshua displayed both masculine and feminine traits but, in fact, it is the feminine traits for which he has been most recently revered: gentleness, compassion, patience, caring for the sick and the poor, love of children. He was most certainly an androgynous archetype in the highest sense of the word.

For the man whom Christians consider to be the only son of God to be portrayed as not only sexual, but androgynous, may seem radical—or, to use my writer friend's word, "repulsive." But, that is what I have been told by many, many women and men with whom I have worked. These are their visions. It gets even more interesting, however.

I asked Ruth (Jeshua's sister), "What else happened at Jeshua and Mary's wedding?" She answered, "Once Jeshua was sealed to Mary Magdalene through the Ceremony of Union, then he would no longer be with the others. Once a sealing takes place, the chakras between the two people are connected. To bring other energies into the field after that would be too disruptive. That understanding has been lost and has been distorted into a rule about adultery. We weren't being told with whom we could be lovers; we were being shown how to keep the energy field strong, dynamic, and balanced. What humans understand about the sacred role of sexuality is very, very limited. It is essential for people to bring balance into their own bodies."

Women and gay men lead the way here, for they are less afraid of intimacy with their feminine sides. Lesbians balance their female bodies with masculine energies. Androgyny is generally easier for them, too.

A Portland woman who recalls having been Cephas (Peter) demonstrated her understanding of Jeshua's mastery of energy. The group was traveling, she said. "We stopped for a little lunch. We're always talking, and somebody asked Jeshua a question:

'How do you heal?' I'm so struck by this. I couldn't hear what he answered. I was just observing. I had to feel him. He really heals people by his being. But he uses some technique, and he's trying to explain the technique." She took some time observing what Jeshua was doing. "OK, what I am experiencing is that he heals by merging with another person. He fully understands we are all one, so it is very easy for him to merge. I can't think of another word. But first I feel him. He prepares for it by expanding his energy. I feel him prepare to answer the question by expanding ... and it takes me in; it takes all of us in. He's trying to show us ... it's not a difficult thing to do ... it is simply *allowing*."

"Please explain what you mean by allowing."

"It's like surrendering into who he really is. He just gets out of his head and he goes into his heart and his essence. He becomes his spirit. You know, we are spirits embodied, so he just taps into his fullness of spirit and expands that out. Then he merges with the person who wants the healing. By doing that, he can participate fully on a very intimate level with them." Cephas laughed heartily.

"You are laughing. What's funny?"

"I still don't get it. He's laughing at me. He says, 'I don't heal you. You heal yourself.' Ohhh, that's it. That's what he does. During the merging, a person feels safe, as if to say, I can go to a place that I have been afraid to go by myself because I have a willing, loving, compassionate soul here with me. So that's what Jeshua does. He gives that safety, and is a witness to who that person is. That is key. That is what we want. We want him to see us. When he acknowledges us, then we can come out because it's safe. He stays merged until we've stabilized. In fact, oftentimes he will charge our energy field too. And he releases so completely and with such honor that it's just a magnificent experience to have joined with him for that period. When he does this with me, I am able to see myself in a new light."

"In a new light. Beautiful," I said.

"[It] was. ... I'm not sure what I'm seeing here, but I'll just say it. Could Jeshua and Cephas have had a sexual relationship? Because that's what I'm seeing."

After probing for a few more details and guiding this client (remember that she is a woman) into her high self for a more objective view, she felt that what she'd seen was accurate. Radical? Well, maybe. But maybe not, when viewed in the context of the times. Jeshua and others had studied in Alexandria and in the Far East. Cephas was speaking about the process of merging energy and joining, both physically and spiritually, and how it was part of his preparation to be both a teacher and healer in the future.

You'll recall what the woman called Magpie had reported. "We [she and Jeshua] are sitting on a bench. ... I'm touching and holding his face, and he is holding my arms. I sometimes get confused when he teaches me about energy. If I keep the energy running in my heart I won't get confused. If the energy runs wild, it gets mixed up with sexual desire, so I'm trying to run it through the heart."

"You are not alone in saying this," I said to Cephas' present-life self. I explained that several people had reported how intimate and sometimes confusing it felt to merge energies with Jeshua and that they had to work to run it through the heart and not confuse it with sexual energy. I also told her I'd heard something about Jeshua and Cephas from a woman who had reported memories of having been Ruth, Jeshua's sister.

In this memory she was looking back to the wedding of Mary and Jeshua. Ruth had said to me, "Cephas was there, but he was very sad and angry. After the ceremony, Jeshua talked with Cephas. He took his hand and then motioned Mary to come over. She put her hand over both of theirs."

"Why was Cephas so sad?"

"They had been intimate," said Ruth. "Jeshua didn't observe any rules about sexuality. He loved who[m] he loved and utilized energy. Merging energy with both men and women brought his physical and emotional body into perfect balance. His masculine side was in perfect balance to his feminine side."

"There are some who suggest Jeshua and John, called 'the Beloved,' were lovers," I said.

"They were also intimate," said Ruth. "But after his marriage to Mary, he was only with her."

"I remember. You explained the sealing of chakras a few weeks ago."

It appears that Bridal Chamber rites (also called the *Sacred Marriage*) were performed at Qumran, which was likely an all-male community. In that event, it isn't a great stretch to imagine Jeshua and John performing that ritual. References to the bride and groom and ancient rituals of the bridal chamber can be found across cultures—Celtic, African, Hebrew, Greek, Asian, etc. "The mythic roots of the Gnostic rite go back to the Garden," writes John R. Mabry, who refers to the *Gospel of Philip* (from the Nag Hammadi Library).

'In the days when Eve was [in] Adam, death did not exist. When she was separated from him, death came into existence.'... For the Gnostic, it is Jeshua's role (as redeemer) to reunite with Sophia [Wisdom], and mythically, to allow humankind with the help of gendered angels to share in that mystery. 'It was for this purpose that his body came into being. On that day he came forth from the bridal bedroom as from what comes to pass between a bridegroom and a bride, which is to say, a unity.'[19]

The modern mystic Andrew Harvey was asked, "Is a realized mystic a kind of archetypal Androgyne?" He answered

Yes. A mature mystic fuses within his or her being the male and the female aspects of the psyche and in so doing consciously realizes the goal of human life, which is to be at once as immanent and transcendent as the divine itself. When the male and female aspects of the inner being fuse they give birth to the child, the Divine Child, the complete being.[20]

Even after reviewing client reports and historical accounts, it still doesn't seem possible to know for sure if the intimacy between Jeshua and others was strictly spiritual or also sexual. Cephas said

---

19. John R. Mabry, "Considering the Gnostic Sacraments" (http://www.essenes.net/considersacr.html), © 1990.
20. Mark Thompson, *Gay Soul: Finding the Heart of Gay Spirit and Nature with Sixteen Writers, Healers, Teachers, and Visionaries* (New York: HarperCollins, 1995), p. 56.

Jeshua would merge his energy with another person. Magpie had to learn to run the energy which she exchanged with Jeshua through her heart, so as not to get it confused with sexual desire. "Merging energy with both men and women brought his [Jeshua's] physical and emotional body into perfect balance," Ruth said.

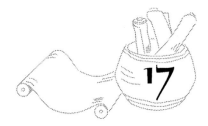

Jeshua and the Female Disciples

*H*annah flew into my office, late for her early morning appointment. She slurped the healthy concoction she always brought with her and announced, "You know, healings were a team effort." The previous week we had just gotten to a point in Hannah's regressions as Myrium (Mother Mary) in which she'd reported that Jeshua was beginning to perform public healings—and we'd run out of time.

"I see you've been thinking about this since we met last week. What did you recall?" I asked.

"We deliberately set ourselves on the speaking platform while members of our group were out in the crowd to hold the energy. [For instance] Cephas and Jeshua might be on the platform and I, in the crowd, would together form an energetic triangle."

In putting together several accounts of the years in which Jeshua taught, there's consensus that in the beginning he did all the teaching and healing of the sick. As time went on, and the crowds grew larger, however, the disciples began to take part, including the women disciples. In mystical circles, the energetic triangle Myrium described is called a *triad*.

Hannah settled into my recliner and went easily into trance. I suggested, "Tell me more about this healing energy, please."

"When we run the energy, my skin will feel electrical, all over. It feels like I'm a lightning rod. I call it down from above, then it goes through my body all the way down to my feet. I then bring it up from below. The two energies then meet in my heart, cross at the heart, and stream out through my hands. It takes a great deal of strength to allow your body to be a lightning rod."

"What is the purpose of running energy in this way?"

"I'm using it to recharge others. I am also healing people. One after another," said Myrium.

"What happens to people during this process?"

"Their energy clears. But, also, the blockages that were in their bodies that kept them from being in health are moving. I see someone using the fingers of his right hand in a way that he hasn't been able to; another with a lame back, healed. [Sighing] I am so tired."

"Is it always this way?"

"Word has gotten out, and there are many people now. And so, right now, it is often like this. Our people take care of us."

"How do they do that?"

"Women bring vessels of drink and oils to massage my arms and shoulders. They bring some nourishing liquid. It contains broth—not animal broth—more than tea, though. It is made from bark and it is nourishing. It tastes very ... substantial. Now I lie back."

"Do the men get equally worn out?"

"I'm looking at Jeshua. He is so much stronger in every way. No, he doesn't. I don't think Cephas does, either, in the same way as I. Not in the same way. Their energy is different. Because I birthed children. Why would that affect me, though? It is just my constitution. Seems to be a difference between men and women. Not that women shouldn't do it. But our bodies are different. This is the body that opens and allows life to come out, and as a result of that our energy [will] run out. So it's important that I take care of the body."

"Please move to another time when you participated in healing."

"A sunshine-y day. We are at a leper colony. Some people don't want us to come here because of the danger of getting the disease. I feel a little bit afraid, but I can't indulge that fear at all. Jeshua says we will be fine and we have a lot of work to do here. I go into my practice [some of which she learned in Tibet]. I first begin to breathe. I'm letting the energy circle in my body. I'm accelerating the pace of the circling. While I do this, I'm also focusing on the chakras and using my breath to help me by breathing stronger—not faster, stronger [she demonstrates]."

"Go on."

"Now the crown is opening; I'm keeping the energy orbiting strongly [breathing deeply]. I'm using my breath to intensify the energy. I have to raise my energy, circulate it fast enough, bring it to a high enough pitch to receive the lightning bolt. We all do this. Then we invite those who wish our help to come forward. Sometimes we work one to one; other times two of us will work with one leper. It depends. So, we really are helping these people. Some are completely healed. We tell them they have allowed God's love to heal them this day. Jeshua always tells people that the ability to heal is within them. We are a lightning rod for the healing energy, only because they don't have enough energy in their sick bodies to channel this energy themselves, and they didn't realize they could. Until today." She smiled, leaned back in the chair, breathed a sigh of serene contentment, and took another drink of her "broth."

In another session, Myrium's daughter, Ruth, told me, "I want to tell you something funny about energy. Well, Jeshua always spoke before the healings started, right? This is one of the first healings I went to, and I was right up front near him, by the platform. When the healings started, the energy just about blew me away—not physically, but I kept getting knocked out of my body. I was very indignant. Later, I said to him, 'That's the last time

I stand next to you, because I want to stay in my body.' Every time he put energy out, I would get blasted out of my body. I stood in the back next time."

After Ruth got used to the energy blast, she began to help. The information she provided under hypnosis proved very consistent with what other women had reported. "Sometimes he calls the disciples to help. He doesn't perform the healing alone. He even calls me. There's an energy to create. He uses me in the emotional healing, and the men for the physical healing. Mary Magdalene also participates. He even asks for people from the crowd to help. He teaches that anybody can use this healing energy. We are all capable of divinity and grace, but we limit ourselves. My brother [Jeshua] explains that through our thoughts and fears we create a dark force. He says if there is darkness within us, we can't be well. He asks if one is ready to let go of darkness. If they are, then healing will occur. If they aren't ready, he tells them to come back later. There is no judgment. He loves the ones who aren't ready as much as the ones who are."

Another incarnation of Mary Magdalene talked about her participation in the healings: "It's about intention. Be the chalice, and what's needed will come. I hold energy; I hold the light. The light comes down and through me. My hands are warm and pulsating ... purple. I'm with an older woman. She's crying ... she's so distressed. She's on her knees, crying into my hands. I touch her. I fill her with love. I know my face is glowing with heat. I bring my hands to my chest and then move them down her back. She breathes."

"Does she say anything?"

"The heart says it all."

"Please move forward."

She made a sweeping gesture. "These are sacred grounds now. We bless the earth and the sky. Then we all gather close. We are so tired ... elated and tired. We have to dance with all the energy. I see Jeshua. It's so good to be back with him at the end of the day."

My friend from Kansas City, whom I visited early in my 1997 road trip, recalled under regression hypnosis that she had been named Anne and had assisted Jeshua during the healings. She said she was twenty-eight and Jeshua was a little older. "My job is to sit with those he has healed and offer more comfort. It is natural for me to do this. I just *love* the people, who are sometimes in great distress afterwards."

"Will you give me an example of how you helped?"

"There was a blind woman. Jeshua touched her eyes, and she could see for the first time in her life. She was overwhelmed with the beauty of everything. I got to be with her as she looked at everything."

"Are there many of you women who participate?"

"Mary Magdalene often works right next to Jeshua. She holds the energy. She's the outward manifestation of the feminine, but masculine and feminine energy [are] balanced within her. Jeshua is also balanced. He told us we all embody both masculine and feminine energy but most of us are out of balance."

"Is this a revolutionary idea?"

"Not for the women; it is for the men. [She looks reflective] Jeshua doesn't want people to get caught up in this phenomenon of healing. He really wants people to know God. He wants us to be aware of the silver cord which attaches [us] to the Divine."

Several other women with whom I have worked also reported that they participated in the healings, sometimes by laying on of hands, at other times by holding energy in the form of geometric patterns. Often they worked quietly, in the background. Almost without exception, women who reported such abilities in their memories are engaged in some type of healing practice now.

One such woman—Brenda, a nurse from Kentucky—has been working with healing energy within a hospital setting. After working with me in hypnoregression and, later, with a teacher, she found herself "into my accelerated experience of healing work." She was called in to work with a two-month-old girl by the name of Emily. Brenda had been recommended to Emily's parents by a woman whom Brenda had helped earlier that year. That woman's dog had been diagnosed with incurable cancer. After three treatments of hands-on healing by Brenda, the cancer went into remission. Brenda told me about little Emily. "She was diagnosed with cardiomyopathy, a serious heart condition. When I first saw her, she was in ICU, hooked up to every kind of monitor imaginable. She was also on a respirator. Almost every inch of this tiny girl was covered with some form of technology."

Brenda said she had felt humble as she approached the hospital—and a little intimidated because Emily's grandfather is a pediatric cardiologist. However, as she entered the small room, "I thought to myself, *I'm going to do whatever I am guided to do for this baby.* I prayed to Jeshua, to my guides, and to the angels, then softly placed my hands on Emily—on her tummy, her leg. I continued to move my hands as I was guided to do. Believe me, I was guided. This baby had many angels surrounding her. Within fifteen minutes, I felt the energy stop flowing, and, intuitively, I knew the session was complete." The following day, Emily was taken off the respirator. She had taken a significant turn for the better.

Brenda returned the next day for another hands-on healing. She was startled to realize how far Emily had been out of her body the previous day. She said, "The moment I saw her, I thought, *Oh, she's back—her spirit, her soul.* This time, Emily looked at me. I was overwhelmed with her beauty and vitality." Within twenty-four hours, Emily was released to go home. Brenda continued working with Emily at home, and at her one-year checkup, Emily had an echocardiogram and other tests which showed her heart to be functioning at ninety-eight percent of normal. Brenda wrote to me, "I now realize, as I enter my third year of doing this work, that I have been blessed to be a vessel for the Christ Energy ... and the miracles continue."

She included a copy of a Christmas note from Emily's mother, who had written: "Brenda, Merry Christmas. You deserve a whole page [in our Christmas letter] just thanking you for all that you have done. I wish everyone had an angel like you. I hope you'll be around to watch Emily go off to college. She'll know that you helped to make sure she got there."

The women whose stories are included in this book are not only remembering abilities from other incarnations, they are being asked by Spirit to add to what was known in the past. They are part of what noted author, lecturer, and futurist Barbara Marx Hubbard refers to as the "Quantum Transition"—as they consciously participate in the evolution *for the betterment* of humankind.

Growing Danger

*M*y clients expressed euphoria at being part of something so phenomenal as Jeshua's mission. The crowds were growing larger with each passing day. "Jeshua is in his glory. He doesn't get tired because he is fulfilling his purpose," said his sister Ruth. "He works with people all day long. He teaches people that all of what they see is natural, not a miracle. He said he isn't special. 'What I can do, you also can do.' This is so new. There is such a hierarchy in Judaism. He teaches that we are all equally endowed." She gasped and put her hand to her mouth. "Now he's done it. The rabbis and priests believe in hierarchy. They are the ones who are blemished. This is threatening." She had a worried look on her face. She shook her head. "This is my fear, not his. I can feel the fear in the crowd, too, though."

Ruth wasn't the only woman who was worried; Mary Magdalene was too. She said, "I don't understand why he is making such grandstanding gestures. I ask him why. He's so loving and placating. [Smiling broadly] He says he's sorry I'm upset and that it scares me, but he feels that now is the time to start

131

reaching as many people as he can. So many people are suffering. He feels he can offer them hope."

I asked, "Are you frightened by his effect on people?"

"People are very attentive. He's charismatic. [She begins to laugh] I'm biased, but people can't help but be drawn in. This is one of the first times he's had so many people listening to him. It's frightening because he's probably going to touch them. It makes me so afraid for him. People won't understand."

The physician from Florida said: "Jeshua says, 'Ma nish-ta-naw ha-lai-law ha-zeh. Blasphemy! You say the words as if they have meaning, but you don't understand what they mean. Why is this night different than all others?'"

"What does he mean, Mary?"

"He is telling the people to stop focusing on the past pain, which is the purpose of the ritual which admonished us never to forget the enslavement in Egypt. He says learning [rote memorization] and following is not the way. Leading is the way." She sat up from a reclining position and began using large gestures. "Each soul leads. He means [it is time to] let go of the ritual that holds on to past grievances. It is time to forgive. To teach a ritual that holds on to anger, blame, and pain is in fact a blasphemy."

Another Mary, this one from Idaho, said, "Jeshua is speaking loudly now. Adamant. He understands our fear but tells us, 'I can't let that bother me.' And so he continues to spread the word of God, not worrying about what will happen to him. And, instead, he gets louder."

"Please move to a later time when you and Jeshua are alone," I prompt her.

"I can't see anything; I can just feel the weightlessness. We are embracing, hands touching. We make love and then we leave our bodies. We are both still in a state of ecstasy. So many feelings. So much pleasure. We have conceived another child. He wants me to understand that the end is close. He wants me to see what is coming, so I won't be afraid. I need to be very strong. It will be a long wait for his return."

"His return? What is he saying about that?"

"He just assures me that nothing will be lost. There is much work to do (she starts to weep softly). He is showing me his mother, as she weeps. I will have to be there for her ... strong."

Sarah of Arimathea said that, some months before Passover, Jeshua gathered his family and friends together. "My father is looking at Jeshua with such love and understanding. Since Jeshua was very young, my father has known who he is. Today Jeshua is telling us that he can see into the future and there are events which will occur that will be difficult. He is stressing that we stay connected. He says, even if things don't make sense and we don't understand, that it is all part of the plan. I can feel Mary Magdalene's pain. She really loves him and is having a difficult time."

I asked Sarah to move forward in time to a few days before Passover. Sarah said Jeshua was not in the city but was expected to arrive soon. She and her father had traveled from their home in Hebron to Jerusalem so that Joseph could attend a special meeting of the Sanhedrin concerning Jeshua and his influence. Sarah walked with her father to the main temple, where the meetings were held. While Joseph changed into his blue robe, she slipped upstairs and discovered a place behind a slit in the stones where she could observe the meeting without being seen. She explained that the council, composed of seventy men representing both geographical regions and sects (Sadducees and Pharisees), sat according to region in a semicircle, with the senior members in front and the newer ones across the back.

"Things are heating up regarding Jeshua. The rabbis are upset. The common people are listening to him; everyone is talking about him. They are concerned for their own position. They feel threatened. My father is just listening; the other men already know how he feels. He understands their fear. Many members of the council are more concerned with authority, ego, and recognition than with spiritual matters. Nothing is decided today; things are too out of control. They adjourn but will reconvene in the morning."

"What happens that evening?"

"We stay with Lazarus, Mary Magdalene, and Martha. As we dine upstairs we discuss what is transpiring. Jeshua is expected any day now, and Father is very anxious to share with Jeshua what the mood is among council members. I want to observe the council meeting again tomorrow, but Father wants me to stay with the women."

"And the next day?"

"He [her father, Joseph] returns that afternoon and says, 'It's no use; I can't put it off. It's time.' He had finally spoken up and asked the council to notice what they sounded like. He said, 'Have you forgotten what this council represents? I am appalled [at] how you are behaving. It is your insecurities getting in the way of listening to Jeshua. He speaks truth. He speaks from the heart, not the intellect. If you would just still yourself and go within, you would know he speaks truth.' Father said some listened, but not enough."

"Go on. What happens next?"

"Father says, 'I'm going to warn Jeshua ... give him a chance to escape.'"

Joseph intercepted Jeshua on the road approaching Jerusalem and delivered his warning. He pleaded with Jeshua to turn back and let things cool down, hoping things would improve over time.

Sarah said, "I realize I am able to see into Jeshua's heart and mind in that moment. I'm seeing Jeshua. He can see what is coming and, with Joseph's warning, now realizes it is real. There is trepidation. A part of him is scared. He will not turn back, however, and now prays for strength. He thanks my father and tells him it is not likely they will see each other again."

Fear and despair swept the household as Joseph delivered Jeshua's farewell.

Myrium reported that one day she was in her garden tending the roses that Jeshua had brought back to her from Persia ten years before. Here, he appeared to her "energetically" [with his astral body]. "He says, 'Mother, it is time.' I say back to him, 'No, it can't be. It can't be.' I plead with him. I say, 'How can you do this to me? I am your mother. How can it be the right time?'"

Myrium's heart was breaking. How she wished things could be different and hoped to find the words which would persuade Jeshua to turn back. The danger was in Jerusalem. Perhaps he could go back to Alexandria; they had sought refuge there when Herod first threatened his life. All Jeshua could do was remind his mother that there was a Divine Plan and that he was prepared to play his part. He assured her that all would be fine. She knew this was true, but that didn't prevent her from being torn apart. She made preparations to hurry to Jerusalem.

Myrium's daughter, Ruth, was in Bethany. She said that Jeshua needed her there to "spy" on the Sanhedrin in nearby Jerusalem. Her report is remarkably similar to Sarah's—which is even more interesting because one woman lives in Florida and the other in Oregon, and they don't know each other.

Ruth said, "I watch and listen. They are in a big room in the Temple, sitting in magnificent chairs. Even though I feel that, for the most part, they are good men, things feel very rigid here. They are discussing Jeshua. The men are afraid that Jeshua is changing the hearts and minds of their members. They are afraid they may lose their status. An older man, Joseph of Arimathea, says this will pass. He is trying to downplay Jeshua's influence. He says, 'This is a good man in touch with the Divine. The more we make an issue of his popularity, the bigger it will become.' Others say it is getting out of hand and that something must be done.

"A younger, clean-shaven man speaks. His name is Nicodemus, and it is obvious he doesn't like Jeshua. [Still] he points out that disagreement with the Sanhedrin or a rabbi isn't a crime. They respect each other's right to opinions. He says, 'Why don't we involve the Romans? Let's give this to the Romans. If we hurt Jeshua, the people will be angry with us. Let's make the Romans responsible.' They all agree that charging Jeshua with blasphemy would not be a crime to the Romans. 'Ah, money,' says

Nicodemus. 'That would upset the Romans.' A story is concocted that Jeshua is inciting the people not to pay taxes. Now, *that* is a crime against the Roman emperor."

"What do you do next?"

"I report back to Jeshua, and he says, 'Aha, now we prepare.' He tells me that he doesn't want others to get hurt; he doesn't want to be arrested in a crowd because that would cause a riot [she heaves a great sigh]. Now I see the seriousness of it all. I feel forty [she is in her early twenties at this time]."

"Please go on. What happens next?"

"Jeshua decides to strategize with the Romans through Judas. Judas is in a different social class from the other disciples, and, with Jeshua's blessing, has cultivated friendships with the Romans. Jeshua doesn't want anyone else to know in order to reduce the risk of inadvertent leaks, which might cause some panic. Jeshua asks Judas to find out if the Romans intend to arrest him, and if so, to let them know that he will go voluntarily."

"How does that go?"

"The Romans tell Judas an arrest is planned. They agree that Judas can lead them to Jeshua, at the place of Jeshua's choosing. They don't want a spectacle either."

I pause briefly here to observe that I've worked with several people who tell a similar story about Judas—that he loved Jeshua and had merely assisted in making the imminent arrest as peaceful as possible. Those who report memories of having been Judas, however, tell a slightly different story, saying there was some kind of emotional betrayal of his beloved friend.

Cephas (Peter) recalled the last time the disciples were together. "I feel uncomfortable with the tension. I feel it spinning tighter inside of me. You know, there is this love/hate relationship people have with Jeshua. They either want him to be incredible or they want him to be nothing. They can't take anything in between. And that really bothers me. So there is this impending sense of doom. Because people can't tolerate him being the Son of God, they are going to make sure he is nothing. He has incredible calm about the whole thing. Incredible calm. I feel his sadness, too."

"He expresses all of the emotions, doesn't he?" I asked.

"He does. He does. And so I feel some nostalgia within him. He is a person who really lives in his heart, and so he is very free with his emotions. He comes to each of us individually and connects deeply, so that he can disconnect freely. And he and I go so far back ..." Cephas drifted off for a few moments, remembering how long they had been friends, then returned to the story. "So there's this big group at the table. It's a very muggy night ... sultry."

"Is everybody here?"

"Everybody's here."

"What's the feeling around the table?"

"It's fun, and it's a little bit quiet. Jeshua does something unusual with each of us. He washes our feet. Jeshua is going around the table, and we are a little puzzled."

"This is not something you've seen before?"

"Well, yes, but we don't understand the intention behind it [tonight]. There is a real serious intention behind what he is doing. He is trying to say something to us that we don't get yet." My client looked puzzled. "It feels very intimate when somebody washes your feet."

"You are remembering him washing your feet?"

"Yes, it's very loving. He does it so singularly. Everybody felt like he alone knew them."

"Yes, I've heard this many times."

"Jeshua doesn't take a long time washing my feet, but it is so sweet and tender and intimate. This is not an act of humility but of great strength. It's exquisite to feel that." He frowned and appeared to be looking across the room where they were gathered. "Yes, this is that meal, because he is telling me that I will deny him, and I'm saying, 'No, I could never do that!' And he says, 'Even you ... it's all right.' And I say that it is never all right. I'm trying to tell him how much I love him and that I will always be with him through thick and thin. I would never betray him. And he says, 'You will.' I feel like he's saying good-bye, and I can't understand why. I feel like crying. I cannot discern why I feel this way. Nothing is happening that is unusual, but it is steeped in emotion. The whole situation is charged, and I'm very jumbled. I feel like I just can't get my feet on the ground."

"Move rather quickly through the next few hours, then."

"So, he takes me and a few of the others to go outside and pray. I am thinking, *Thank God! I gotta get out of here!* At least I can go pray and meditate and be by myself for a little while. This will be good."

"You're calming down."

"I feel outside of myself; it's very strange. I'm feeling so detached. So we are all praying, and I fall asleep. He comes over. He shakes me and says, 'Cephas, come.' He's sad. Jeshua is sad, and it is so still. Can you feel the stillness?" Cephas asked me.

"Yes actually, I can," I said, and I meant it. My usually busy street was silent and there were no officemates stirring in the hall. No phones were ringing in the distance. It was utterly quiet.

"Do you know why he's sad?" I asked.

"He keeps saying he has a purpose, and he needs to follow it. He is divided in his feeling about it."

"Yes ... understandable. Let's move forward again."

"Well, we went back. The rest are still in this room [where they dined]. Maybe we all agreed to meet back here later. I'm feeling kind of woozy, like I could have stayed in the garden a lot longer. I need to sleep tonight, I am so tired."

"What happens next?"

"These people come in the door and they arrest Jeshua. His eyes meet mine just as they are putting these things on his arms. He looks into my eyes as if to say, 'So be it.' I don't panic; I feel confusion about what's going on."

"Well, do the men who arrest Jeshua say why, or say anything?"

"They're taking him to see somebody—one of the officials."

"Do they say who?"

"It's Pilate."

"Had you seen this coming?"

"Not really ... I don't know. ... on some level I did, because I'm not surprised and I'm not panicking."

"And you could see that he wasn't panicking."

"No, he wasn't panicking. He just said, 'Yes, so be it.'"

I'm not a biblical scholar; and, in fact, I have deliberately not read the Bible during the last ten years so that I would bring no preconceived beliefs about what would happen next into my clients' sessions. As a child, I heard Bible stories and I took one course, "The Bible as Literature," in college, so I really don't know enough to compare what my clients report with what the Gospels state. But when Cephas said that Jeshua's arrest took place in the room where they had dined and not in the Garden, I did realize this detail was at odds with tradition. I wondered if it mattered.

In her latest book, *Beyond Belief: The Secret Gospel of Thomas,* Elaine Pagels says,

> [S]ome historians, having compared the *Gospel of Mark* (written 68 to 70 C.E.) with the gospels of Matthew and Luke (c. 80 to 90) and then with that of John (c. 90 to 100), have thought that John's gospel represents a transition from a lower to a higher Christology—and increasingly elevated view of Jesus. [This latter is the view which was finally] enshrined in the Nicene Creed [in the fourth century].[21]

In other words the story of who Jeshua was had been changed, along with his essential messages, in a couple of profound and significant ways: firstly, from his being a fully realized but human being who taught that God was within all people — to being the *only* Son of God — and secondly, from his teaching that God loves all — to God's love is dogmatically conditional. Furthermore, there are many details within the four accepted Gospels which differ from one another. Therefore, I have decided that details aren't the central focus. The meaning that accessing this material has for my clients and for my readers is what matters. What is interesting, however, is that my clients' reports seem to agree more with the earlier Gospels than with John's Gospel, and much more with the excluded *Gospel of Thomas,* part of the Nag Hammadi Library.

---

21. Elaine Pagels, *Beyond Belief: The Secret Gospel of Thomas* (New York: Vintage Books, 2004), p. 45.

Ruth picked up the story and reported what the women were doing. "I was with Mary Magdalene and Martha and their brother [in Bethany] when we got word that the Romans had taken Jeshua. There was a lot of confusion afterwards. We sent for Mother. [She begins to sob] I need her."

"Please move forward to when your mother arrives. I can see that you know things are very serious at this point."

"I say to my mother, 'They are going to take his life! You knew, didn't you? Is this why you weren't going to come for Passover this time?' [Ruth sighs] Mother just looks at me, puts out her arms and holds me. There is nothing to say."

Martha served tea with honey as the women kept vigil over the next several hours.

"Mother is quiet," said Ruth. "I have never seen her quiet, and that worries me. Cephas and the others are frantic, and that is making me more upset. Oh, I see. Mother is in a different state—she is with Jeshua. I'm not able to do that right now. I'm too afraid."

"Please go on, Ruth."

"I run from the house and into the garden, crying and praying, 'Dear Jeshua, Elijah, all my masters, please help me with the fear. I can't change what is happening, but I need help to change how I'm looking at this.' Jeshua taught us that when we are completely connected to the Divine, there is no fear. I need to free myself from fear so I can get through what is coming. I want to be with Jeshua in the way Mother is. I want to be of comfort to my brother." She exhaled and her pale skin regained some color.

"I can see that you are breathing easier now."

"I'm feeling better. There is light around me. I feel I am in the space of love."

I was reluctant to disturb her in this space of love and remained silent for several minutes. Finally, I prompted, "Please move forward in time."

"I walk back into the [Bethany] house. I see Cephas and the others. I can see their fear, how guilty and helpless they are feeling. I think to myself, *You can't help. Don't blame yourselves. That is not what he wants.*"

"Do you know what is happening to Jeshua?"

"No. It is hard not knowing. No one is permitted to see him, not even Mother."

"What happens next?"

"Nicodemus comes to the house to give us news. He tells us that Jeshua had gone before the council, and it hadn't gone well. He said Jeshua was stubborn. He wouldn't admit to the charges, but he didn't deny them either. He didn't say he wasn't God, but then he didn't say he was. [She holds her stomach] I feel sick. Nicodemus takes Cephas aside. I can't hear what they are talking about, but I see that Cephas looks scared. I figure he thinks he might be arrested, too. Cephas is leaving the house."

"Do you think you are all in danger of being arrested?"

"Women aren't considered a threat. I don't feel personally in danger."

"How is your mother doing?"

"Mother continues to be in a trance state, refusing food or drink. You remember that we Essenes can literally leave our physical bodies and travel great distances? Mother is with Jeshua now."

Ruth said that Cephas left the house in fear after Nicodemus' visit. Cephas, however, reported that he left the house with the intention of finding out what was happening to Jeshua: "They won't let us in. I'm skirting the place where Jeshua is [being held], trying to get news about what's going on." Cephas sucked in his breath and began to cry. "A little girl comes up. She's about twelve or fifteen and she says, 'Oh, look! You're one of ... aren't you one of his followers? Aren't you one of his friends?' [It's as if she were saying], 'Look, everybody, look at this guy!' And then I just panic. I am just terrified. And I say, 'No, I'm not.'" Cephas appeared to me to be looking around, his head swinging back and forth in the recliner in my office. "And then a crowd gathers. This simmer starts to boil. 'Oh, yes, you are,' [they chant]. They are shoving, and they're stabbing their fingers at me. They are saying, 'I've seen you! You've been with him! You know him!' And I say to myself, *I gotta get out of here.* I say, 'No!' and I run."

I encouraged this client to step outside of the scene for a moment to breathe and calm down.

"Why were you terrified?"

"I was thinking I was going to be tortured in some way. They were very angry, like a mob."

"You were needed to carry on the work. I'm glad you got away."

"Well, I feel awful about it, because before that girl confronted me, I could feel Jeshua. And he wasn't worried. He was very calm. And so I was confident that he was going to be released. I wasn't really paying attention to the crowd and how they felt. But when the crowd gathered, my whole calm shattered. I wasn't with Jeshua any more; I was with myself, and I was terrified. I didn't have the depth and strength and the calm that he had."

Imagine carrying the guilt of denying one's association with Jeshua for two thousand years! And, in addition, judging oneself against a master. Most of us do that. The irony is that masters, such as Jeshua, see into the heart and soul with compassion, not with judgment. I said to her, "I imagine that Jeshua would have said to Cephas, 'I'm sad for you that fear caused you to act contrary to your beliefs, and I am amazed that you expected yourself to be perfect. Please forgive yourself.'"

This client did some very good work that day. She forgave her Cephas self.

Finally, the verdict was made public. Jeshua had been accused of blasphemy by the Sanhedrin and convicted of sedition by the Romans. Myrium said that the sentencing was conducted in public and that she was there.

"Only two days ago he entered Jerusalem in triumph. He went from the top of the mountain to being spat upon. He is sitting on a platform, being ridiculed and humiliated, and spat upon. It is devastating. Horrible. The sentence is pronounced: crucifixion!"

Mary Magdalene also relived that horrible time. I'd prompted: "Mary, please go back to the last time you were with Jeshua prior to his physical death."

"I cried, 'A-do-nai e-chad. A-do-nai e-chad.' Jeshua said to me, 'Shalom, Shalom Sheinah.' 'Shalom alechem, Jeshua.[22] I love you.'

[Sobbing] He dies tomorrow. I am angry with God. I am powerful, but God is a million, million, million times more powerful than I. He could stop this! Damn you, Father!" Mary was racked with emotion and cried out, "Jeshua! You are flesh of my flesh. I love you. I was so afraid they were going to kill you. And now ... " Her head dropped. She was flooded with despair. "I was born with the acceptance. I have the knowledge, and I know that I was sent to try to protect him. But I can't protect him. Father, I'm sorry. I couldn't protect him. Father, I am sorry."

Suddenly, her voice deepened, her posture changed, and she appeared to start channeling. In a calm voice, she said: "Mary loved Jeshua. She really *loved* him. She could not feel that love unless she had that pain. God would not interfere. What is happening will create something better. Mary will be with Jeshua in spirit. A tiny bit of Jeshua will be in everybody, and it will be easier now. She can get through this, but we all have to work together." She looked radiant.

"I feel so foolish. He lit a little flame in everyone. He will never die. I am ready."

---

22. "God is One, God is One," Mary Magdalene said. "Peace, peace, Beautiful One," Jeshua replied. "Peace be unto you, Jeshua."

WOMEN AT THE CROSS

After Jeshua's sentence was announced, the women gathered together. They needed to prepare themselves before walking to Golgotha, where the crucifixion would take place.

Ruth said, "Jeshua needs us to remain in divine space and not slip into seeing him in pain. His body is not what he is. We focus on each other and encircle him with love. He needs us as much as we ever needed him. He taught us we have a choice: We can live in pain and fear or slip into the stream of the All, which is pure love. We made that choice for us and for him. We can go now [to Golgotha]."

In spite of Ruth's confidence and Mary Magdalene's determination to remain in spiritual space and not slip into fear and pain, they still suffered greatly as they watched the Romans nail Jeshua to a cross.

"It's time," said Mary. "I see him on the cross. It's OK. This is the way ... [her face is stoic] I have prepared. This is not an ending; it's a continuing, a releasing." She sobbed and covered her face. "I don't want to stay here without you. Don't make me stay here. I want to go too!" The sobbing continued and then she nodded her head. "I know, I know. It's harder than I thought. He'll never hold me again, not like that. I know, I know." Mary was torn between what she knew through her preparation for this day, and how she felt. "I don't want to do this without him," she cried. Then she sighed, "I know. You'll always be with me. I know I'll see you."

Almost every person I've worked with who has past-life connections to Jeshua reports this event, and without exception they report the expected feelings of horror and outrage—but not so expected are their heartfelt expressions of guilt.

In 1998 I was on a lecture and workshop tour in the Northwest. One day was particularly busy, as I had private sessions all day at the Visions Gallery in Bellevue, and I had a lecture that evening at a book shop called Stargazer. I had been given directions to Stargazer, but somehow I got lost. I didn't have a cell phone, nor did I see any signs of a pay phone when I stopped my car just ten minutes before I was scheduled to speak. I asked my guides for help.

"I don't know where I am or where I need to be, but I have ten minutes to get there," I whispered. I heard a voice tell me I was very close. The voice instructed me to drive to the intersection and turn right, to keep driving and keep looking right. In spite of my feeling that I was going in the wrong direction, I soon spotted the building on the right. It was small and rather set back from the road. I might have driven right by it, had I not been watching. I breathed a sigh of relief and gratitude as I hurried in the door right on the dot of seven o'clock. I apologized to my hosts for any worry I might have caused them and walked into the meeting room. It was filled mostly with women. My lecture was "Mary Magdalene: Archetype of the Divine Feminine." Midway through my lecture, I asked if anyone in the group had past-life memories of having been Mary. One woman confidently threw her hand in the air. I was about to ask her if she'd be willing to share some of her recollections when another one snuck her hand into the air. Then several more hands went up, and the group let out a collective gasp.

"How can this be?" a woman asked. "How can there be more than one?"

I said, "You are here because of a strong affinity to Mary Magdalene. Everywhere I've been—in settings like this one—I've found several women who report they believe they were Mary in a past life." I have come to use the term *aspect of Mary* as a means of discussion. For those who accept the concept of soul records, or Akashic Records, it might make sense that if one has the right vibrational key, one can access any records. Dr. Jean Shinoda Bolen, the great Jungian psychiatrist, in her book *Goddesses in Everywoman* (HarperCollins, 1993), wrote that at different points in a woman's life different archetypal energies are active. Bolen used the ancient Greek goddesses as her examples. However, other archetypes abound, and Mary Magdalene is highly active as an archetype right now.

That evening, I invited the women with access to this archetype to share their experiences—and they did, with an out-pouring of grief and guilt. One woman said, "I feel like there must have been something I could have done to save his life," and she began to weep. Another woman agreed with her, and then another. "I didn't do enough!" they cried. One woman said she blamed herself "that things got so messed up later."

"Listen to me," I said. "I've been collecting pieces of this story through the collective experiences of people like you, and I'm telling you that almost everyone feels guilt or anger, usually both. Each one seems to carry some kind of imprint that they didn't do enough. Of course, what follows is that if they had done it right, the world would be a different place today. All I can say to you is that Mary did everything she could do, for Jeshua and for the mission. People exercised their free will and, yes, things did get messed up. What matters now is how you live this lifetime you are now living. There's a reason you have incarnated at this time. I recommend you take the time to discover why. I agree with Reinhold Niebuhr, who wrote, 'Nothing worth doing is completed in one lifetime, therefore we must be saved by hope.'"

"What kinds of things are you doing in this lifetime?" I asked those grieving women, and I wasn't surprised to learn how many were in helping professions today. I ended the lecture by guiding a visualization back to that time. I asked the participants to see themselves grieving the loss of the great Teacher and to see themselves today, living his simple messages: love one another; do not judge others; God is within each person.

As usually happens at book signings and lectures, I was asked if I had memories of having known Jeshua. I shared my recollection of having been a teacher at the monastery in Tibet where Jeshua went to study. Because we had focused so much on the crucifixion that evening, I told them what I remembered about that time. The following paragraph is an excerpt from my own past-life regression.

"During meditation, Jeshua came to me (in spirit) and said, 'My beloved teacher, the time has come. Will you extend your energy to me and hold me as I remember who I am?' I traveled with my spirit mind to him and remained with him three days. At the final hour, I joined with his family and his friends and all who loved him, and we formed a womb of love around and above him. We helped him lift from that body and rejoiced with him. The sky was filled with angels."

Ruth reported in whispered tones, "Peace. It is over. There is no sorrow. We sit there for some time, awaiting the release of the body. Joseph [of Arimathea] has a place waiting. They release the body to him, and we follow. Mary Magdalene, with the help of some other women, anoints his body with herbs and oils. They lovingly wrap his body with cloth, place him in the tomb, and then pile stones to seal the opening."

I have revisited this scene a hundred times since people began relating their stories to me of their remembrances of Jeshua's death. I'm always so moved and drained by the time I get to here that I find myself in some kind of suspension—like that pause after a brilliant aria has been sung and before the audience begins clapping, or the quality in the air long after a gong has been sounded: still something there, not silence, but too soon to speak.

It's my experience that almost anyone who reports a past life of having known Jeshua either starts here, with the crucifixion, or reports it during their regression session, even if it is only a one-hour session. Jeshua's death seems to be the defining experience for most of them. I suppose that shouldn't surprise me. Birth and death are defining moments for us all. However, Jeshua's death goes much beyond the personal—it is archetypal.

Following the lecture on Mary Magdalene in Portland, Oregon, in July 1998, I received a letter from a young woman with Magdalene memories. She wrote of a deeply spiritual experience involving the Black Madonna at a church she visited in Poland in 1988. She wrote: "Now, I feel like something has fallen into place in the most mysterious way ten years later. I think I somehow knew that this particular painting ... represented the lost feminine in Christianity, and that I had never seen it anywhere else and never would again. And that it was for my own lost faith that I mourned." She enclosed the following poem, which she had composed after my lecture:

The Widow Jerusalem

It does not seem
possible that it was
only yesterday that
I held you in my
arms heavy hot
and fragile flesh that never
made your heart more
real to me or the path inside you
slow down
I knew you were
beyond me when
you closed your
eyes to the night when
you made your breaths
deliberately your own and
not that single breath we
create in love the god
within you and the

god within me
cannot make this any easier I cannot
fathom earth life
without you
except that the map
in the stars cannot be
altered by human love you
lived in my body before I met you and
you will love in my body after you
have gone since we found the proof of
our existence in the other I
cannot die with you and
I thought myself strong
then when I held you in my arms when
I held you as you pretended
to sleep

—Tonya S. McCulley
July 1998

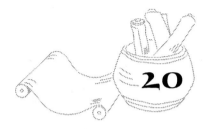

RESURRECTION

*R*uth was bereft. Her beloved brother was dead. She spoke as if she were numb. "We are at Mary Magdalene's house. It is not long after the anointing of the body." She sat up and spoke with more animation. "Somebody tells us something has happened at the tomb. Three of us—me, Mary Magdalene, and Martha—hurry to see what has happened. The Roman guards are still there. The rocks we used to seal the tomb have been moved. I see a glow. [She gasps] An angel. A beautiful being." She spent a few moments to take this in. "He says he is the Archangel Michael, and he's telling us not to be afraid. He says there are messages for each of us. For me he says, 'Don't worry about your brother; he is with us.' Mary and Martha see him too. I could *feel* as well as see him. Even though it was still dark outside, a golden glow made it seem like day.

"When we finally left the tomb, the soldiers knew something had happened. They could tell something awesome had happened. One is falling on his knees. They are transfixed. I can see they are looking at us. The angel is behind us ... no wonder.

They see him too. They are falling on their knees. One lays his sword down and follows after us. [Laughing] It's not hard to make converts that way. He's coming with us. This is serious to leave his post. This is a big thing.

"We are excited—hurrying back, the soldiers following. Someone asks what happened, and we are trying to explain. Cephas says, 'Now tell me again.' Someone new would come, and we'd tell it all over again.

"The message to Mary Magdalene was 'Jeshua wants you to carry on his work ... his teachings. He is not gone. He will appear within three days. Tell Cephas he will be back.'"

Three days pass.

A client who reports she was "the other Mary" said, "Jeshua told us to be strong, but I'm afraid. I feel ... [she sobs] I have to believe, but I'm sad and I'm afraid. I have to trust that he will be here. I'm with Mary. She has more faith, and she comforts me. I feel stronger around her. [Smiling] She has news. The tomb is empty. It's true! He lives. There was so much sadness and now joy."

Clients report the resurrection much as it was reported in the New Testament, and even more, as it is reported in a Gnostic text, *The Gospel of Mary*. Mary Magdalene is the first to discover that Jeshua's body is not where it was left and the first to whom he appears in etheric form. Mary had told the other disciples that Jeshua wanted them to carry on the work, but they were afraid that if they began to preach they might also be killed.

> Then Mary arose, embraced them all, and began to speak to her brothers: "Do not remain in sorrow and doubt, for his grace will guide, protect, and comfort you."[23]

Ruth said, "Cephas is just beside himself. Now he is telling it. He could hardly explain what happened. Now Cephas is settling down; he's [re]gaining his composure. Cephas doesn't usually lose it. Jeshua has visited them several times. We asked, 'What did the Master say? What did he share with you?' Several started talking

---

23. *The Gospel of Mary* (Chapters 5, 9), NHL.

at once. We are jabbering away. We agree to be quiet so we can hear what Cephas has to say. 'I saw him. There was a glowing light all about him. He was magnificent. The message was to carry on, go out and talk to the people. Give the messages I was giving. Heal those in need of healing.' He had a private message for Cephas. He chose him for his strength and for the way he can relate to people. He said, 'You are my strength, my channel, Cephas.'"

Cephas said, "He appeared to us several—at least two times, no, at least three that I can distinctly recall. What was so interesting was how he felt. I always participated with him through feeling his energy. When I saw him [in the resurrected state] I thought, *Well, yes, he is here but he is gossamer.* His emotional body is not intact at all. It is not even a part of him at all. He has ascended. He has released his emotional body, and so it is like he is here in his higher-self form, without the attachment of his emotional body. So there wasn't anything to hold on to. When I open to connection, a big piece of me can attach to an emotional body. When one doesn't have that emotional body, it is like trying to hold onto gossamer fabric. One would float off, because there is nothing sticky about it. He had lost the stickiness of the human condition. Us humans identify with the stickiness, which holds all the pain, all the human condition. And the higher self ... I felt the truth of that so strongly; it was like my whole body just shook with it."

Ruth agreed. "We now understand there is no death. Only change. Only transformation. I remember how Cephas looked at the rest of us in the room. Huge tears in his eyes. So much love. He was a loving soul. A bit gnarly, not usually seen like this, the compassion. I knew for sure my brother had spoken to him. Cephas had changed."

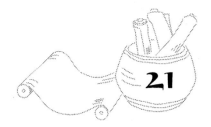

THE ALIENATION OF THE WOMEN

*M*artha, Sarah, Anne, Ruth, and Magpie had all been disciples, and now they were fully prepared and eager to become apostles. According to *The Dialogue of the Savior,* another book from the Nag Hammadi discoveries, Mary Magdalene appears to have been the one whom Jeshua intended to lead the work. She was one of three disciples chosen by Jeshua, along with Thomas and Matthew, to receive special teaching. Furthermore, this text indicates that Jeshua praised Mary above the other two, saying, "She spoke as a woman who knew the All."

As we shall see, in spite of Jeshua's influence, the women and men who had followed him began to struggle with the women's entitlement to be involved in the new organization. Jeshua left no specific instructions. He taught that everyone was a leader. While Jeshua was alive, he encouraged women like Magpie, the young woman whose feet he had washed, to recognize their value and to take their place as equals with men. Some women, such as his mother, his sister, and his wife, were already awake. Others, like Martha, woke up to the fact of their power, and it appeared that once awakened, they stayed awake.

In *The Messengers,* Paul described the early efforts of Jeshua's followers to spread what he called the Good News. He said they established quarters in Bethany and recruited people to join them. He identified Cephas as the leader. Paul wasn't interested in becoming involved with them, even though Cephas had invited him. He disagreed with some of the things they were saying, such as, "Unless you accept Jeshua as the Messiah, you cannot have salvation." Paul argued the unfairness of that teaching because it implied one had to be a Jew or convert to Judaism. He also objected to the fear they were putting in people's hearts and to their alienating the Pharisees.

While some people accepted Cephas as the leader, others decided that James, Jeshua's brother, should be the leader. I wondered why, if Jeshua had designated Mary Magdalene to be his successor, was I not hearing that from my regression clients. What role *were* the women playing in the aftermath of Jeshua's death?

During one session, I asked Ruth how things were going. She groaned. "It's not good. They started from day one messing things up. I get so angry at this. I really do. Mary and I talk about it all the time. The three of us—Mary, Mother, and I—are all so horrified. We can't seem to talk them out of it. The men do not understand. They are so ... almost naive. It is so frustrating!"

"What are you most frustrated about?"

"James. My brother James. Some of the men thought he should be the new leader because he's Jeshua's brother. But he's taking Jeshua's words and ... [she cries hard] turning them around. He's making it sound like you have to follow him ... instead of following the inner person. Jeshua didn't say that. He didn't say, follow me to heaven. He said, follow yourself. And they are having people pay—they are making people give them all their money. Things like that." She was weeping before me as if her heart were broken. "Mother and Mary are so upset. We are trying to salvage as much as we can. We've hidden some things so he won't be able to destroy them, but I don't know what is going to happen. He's not the only one, though. The men won't talk against him. They keep following him even though they have to know it's not true. I don't know why they are doing this!"

"How is James treating his mother?"

"Not respectfully. He says that she doesn't know anything, but he knows that she does. She's a great healer, and he won't listen to her. Timothy got so angry at him he told him he wasn't ... he wasn't going to acknowledge him as his [spiritual] brother any more. Mother and I told him that wouldn't help, but he just left. He won't come back. He's going to go back and live in the community. The family is really broken up."

"James wasn't very interested in Jeshua's work before his death, was he?"

"No, but it was because he was jealous. He would mock him. One of the uncles is in partnership with him ... from my father's side. I don't know why." (James' story is told in the next chapter.)

According to the women, it appears things hadn't improved by the second year. "He's been dead for two years, and it's all gone," said Jeshua's mother, Myrium, who bordered on hysteria in this session. "The work is all gone. [Gasping for air, her crying becoming sobbing] He was killed ... they killed him before his work was complete! The work is all gone."

"You are still deep in grief. Where are you now?"

Still crying, Myrium swallowed and sighed. "I can't ... I can't ... well, I can smell something. The smell of wet, like being in a sandy damp cave. There are men who are raving like they know what is going on ... and they don't!"

"Who are these men?"

"Oh. I see Cephas [sighing] and the others ... and they don't get it!" She looked tortured. "I had hopes that the work would go on even though Jeshua died. And ... [gasping] ... it isn't. Not in the way he wanted it to. There's a group of women that understood."

In *The Gospel of Mary*, we are told that after the crucifixion the disciples were terrified. Several asked Mary Magdalene to encourage them by sharing what Jeshua had secretly told her. But instead of listening to her, Cephas attacked Mary, asking how it was possible that the Teacher told a woman secrets he didn't tell the men.

"Did he really choose her, and prefer her to us?" Mary wept and said to Cephas, "My brother, what are you thinking? Do you believe I invented my visions? Do you think I would lie about Jeshua?" Levi broke in to defend Mary. "Cephas, you've always been hot tempered and now you are criticising a woman, just as our adversaries do. Yet if Jeshua held her worthy, who are you to challenge her? Surely the Teacher knew her well. That is why he loved her more than us."[24]

The insisting that the men accept Mary Magdalene's birthright and her status was short-lived. Myrium cried, "I'm in despair. I birthed him ... but I didn't birth him for this. He was born to be this burst of light ... to bring light, radiant light ... and it was not understood, and no amount of screaming from me is doing any good. Nobody is listening. Nobody is hearing anything. I feel like they are saying, 'You are just a mother.'" Her face was red, her fists clenched, grief turned to anger. The men did not listen to the women.

As G.W. Hardin edited this book, he would from time to time ask me how I felt about what my clients were reporting. There were times when I wept with them or laughed with them, but often I was simply a detached witness, as I had been trained to be. In regard to Myrium's despair, he asked me, "As a woman, was this difficult for you to hear?" I agreed that it was—as difficult as watching the nightly news hearing that some very hard-won rights for women are in jeopardy; or when I hear that another mother's child has died in a war against which I protested; or another woman is murdered by her jealous lover. Yes, I am angry, and yes, I do grieve with Myrium and Mary Magdalene.

A few years had passed, and by now Paul had returned from Damascus and was helping. I asked Ruth how things had changed. "It's still frustrating. Mother said that at least Paul brought some

24. *The Gospel of Mary* (Chapter 9), NHL.

organization. There were a couple of things he got corrected because things frustrated him, too. But it was difficult to change a lot because it had already been set. He did bring more organization."

"Do you stay in contact with Cephas?"

"Because of his relationship with Jeshua, he and Mary have become very close. They weren't at first. Cephas was very jealous of Mary, but he has changed a lot. I didn't have much to do with the others, and James and I didn't talk. We were very distant."

I asked Ruth to move forward in time. She was now in her late twenties and busy with her two-year-old twins. She was concerned about her mother. "She went back to Jerusalem again and tried to talk to them. She is so tired, and I tell her she can't do that any more. She is so, so tired. I tell her we have to let it go. We are not going to be able to get it back on track so that's when we make the decision not to try anymore."

The woman with Cephas' memories said, "It is really interesting that in this [present] lifetime I abhor politics, and I got very political in that lifetime. When I remembered my death in my lifetime as Cephas and I looked back, I believed that I stayed true to my beliefs and my convictions, but I was so saddened by the realization that even when you stay in integrity, the ways of the world can still make it different than what you had hoped it to be. It got very political. ... I had to deal with Paul. I had to deal with the factions, the diversity."

"What were the politics in dealing with Paul?"

"What happened, in my understanding, is that Jeshua came to Paul on the road to Damascus and asked him to be part of the group. Before that, he had scorned us. He was an upper-class, educated businessman and a Roman citizen, who didn't hold that we knew what was going on. How could we, a bunch of people like us [know anything]? After he was called by Jeshua to participate, he wanted to do it his way. He was a very strong person, and his way was the truth, period. So, by gathering numbers of followers, we gained some leverage. But I always felt that Myrium, me, and John—gentle, soft-spoken John—were like ringleaders in a particular faction. Paul wanted to prescribe the way Jeshua's teachings should be shared and, while he had exchanged lots of conversations with Jeshua—many intimate, deep, and philosophical conversations—he hadn't been taught it the way we who had lived with him for years had. So there were differences that were hard to resolve."

She continued, "And we kept doing the healing work because that seemed to bring Jeshua's teaching most close to people's hearts. That was my impression of what happened, and I have a lot of worries about the integrity of it because it kept shifting with these factions that seemed to get out of control."

Paul, as reported in *The Messengers*, made a historic decision that women would no longer hold positions in the priesthood of the new religion developing around Jeshua's teachings. This was during the development of the church in Laodicea. One of the important leaders there was Lucius, a close and respected friend of Paul's. Lucius fell in love with a Roman woman by the name of Vesta, with whom he had two children. The problem was, Lucius was married to Mariah. Paul was alarmed that Lucius and Vesta's affair, as well as the sexual activities of other missionaries, would destroy the work of making converts. Paul decided to solve the problem with a new policy.

> I insist on it. Anybody I appoint from this time, if he is single, unmarried, he must commit himself to being celibate from that point on. Otherwise I won't appoint him. Also, I don't think we should have women in those positions of responsibility because they're coming in too close of contact with the men. They're getting involved in relationships, and many of these women are married.... I won't appoint any more women. Women will no longer, as far as I'm concerned, hold positions of priesthood.[25]

After Paul told me of his new policy to eliminate women from positions of responsibility and to forbid them future responsibility because of sexual relationships occurring among his missionaries, I rather perversely asked him, "Why not keep

25. *The Messengers* (Skywin, 1996), pp. 282-283.

the women in power and eliminate the men?" Of course, this wasn't a fair question. Paul did answer, however.

Our society," he said, "is one which generally looks to the men for the major decision making. If we had said that women could be the leaders rather than the men, this would have deterred many, many men from becoming followers. ... I did not consider that as an option."[26]

Paul instituted the rule of celibacy for single men in positions of authority in the Church. He did not forbid marriage but did require that married men have sex only with their wives. It was not until the fourth century that the policy of celibacy was extended to cover married priests, and it was later still that priests were not allowed to marry at all.

Paul's new policy (because of these matters of the heart among Lucius; his wife, Mariah; and his mistress, Vesta) combined with Paul's drive to keep credibility high and threw everything out of balance. Placing his actions in historical context, I don't condemn Paul for these decisions. I love and admire this great man, and I believe he did his best to do Jeshua's bidding to help spread the Good News to as many people as possible. He made marketing decisions. But he acted alone. He did not collaborate, even with his closest friends and colleagues, all of whom would be affected by these decisions. Women were stripped of power in the emerging movement, now called "Christianity" as it moved from Jerusalem to the emerging heart of power in the world: Rome.

Sarah of Arimathea had said, "When Paul took women out of the movement, the balance was destroyed. That didn't happen with Jeshua; he held women in high esteem. The movement left Jerusalem for Rome. It is in the men's hands now. The Good News now must fit into their patriarchal paradigm. I die angry."

---

26. Ibid. p. 284.

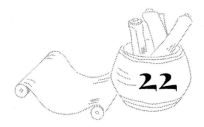

THE STRUGGLE OF JAMES,
THE RELUCTANT FIGUREHEAD

*M*yrium's son James, the second-born, had headed up one
of the factions about which Cephas had been concerned.
Had James' jealousy of his brother Jeshua influenced the way he
would carry on? Myrium believed it had. In fact, she began to
blame herself for how antifemale the Catholic Church eventually
became and how devoid of a Mother God the Protestant religion
is today. She speculated that James may have acted out his anger
towards her in this way and wondered if she could have
mitigated her younger son's jealousy by treating James as
someone special, like Jeshua—perhaps James would have been a
part of the group early on. The Church that James headed might
have been different then, too.

Mother and son relationships are often complicated. My client
Myrium was looking at an age-old story, the jealousy of one
brother towards another. While Myrium had her theory, Ruth also
wondered why her brother behaved the way he had. Ruth said
that James had twisted Jeshua's words and used them to put fear
into the hearts of people in order to get them to contribute money

to the organization. Ruth cried that James was not treating her mother with respect.

I was fortunate during my visit to Florida to find another piece of the story: a woman I will call Karen, who has the memories of the very man the others were discussing. She learned I was in town and arranged to meet with me. Karen is an attractive, gentle, energetic woman, who manages two careers—as a business-woman and as a past-life therapist. Through Karen's memory, James reported the following:

"All the disciples hounded me for two years to be the head. I wasn't prepared, but it's tribal tradition. It's like a politician gets hounded."

"What was your response when they first approached you?" I asked.

"My heart is racing. 'I'm not a leader,' I object. But the disciples tell me they will take care of things. They say, 'You are his brother; people will look up to you.' But I'm nowhere near where he was. I try to tell them ... *beg* for us to go into the wilderness for forty days, like Jeshua did. But people wanted the healings ... *demanded* them." James felt in his heart it would have been better to prepare, but they didn't spend the forty days in prayer. He said Jeshua didn't give enough instructions before he was killed and that the splits in the early Church came about because of the people's heritage.

"[We were trying to incorporate the philosophies of] Pharisees, Sadducees, Essenes, and, later, pagans. There were bound to be conflicts about how to do things, how to live your life. We all would filter the 'Good News' through our own beliefs, each vying for control. Finally, the strongest prevailed—Paul and Peter, sometimes John. I was outwardly strong, but people didn't see how weak and afraid I really was. You know how men put up a facade?"

Ruth had questioned James' practice of demanding money from converts. I thought perhaps James fell back on what he knew traditionally as he took on the role of leader. It appears he may have organized matters based upon the practices at Qumran. The historian Josephus, who actually spent time at Qumran Monastery, wrote, "They hold all their goods in common. New members must surrender their property to the order, and all must contribute to it their earnings."[27]

I returned to the typed transcripts of Ruth's sessions to see if she had said anything else about the teachings being changed or distorted. She said converts were told it was a *sin* not to give up their money. I recalled Ruth's indignation over anyone's claiming Jeshua talked about sin. I had said to Ruth, "In my time, many people believe that the reason Jeshua died was to save us from our sins."

"Jeshua was murdered! He *lived* for us. He didn't *die* for us. He was killed before the work was firmly anchored. My brother didn't teach about sin. He taught love and compassion. They got it wrong!"

When certain apostles, after long debate, finally decided to allow gentiles and heathens to convert to the Good News without first becoming Jews, James split off from the others. Paul said this group was called the Ebionites, or "poor men." Some think the Ebionites were also called the Nazarenes. They were ultra-conservative Jews who considered Paul an apostate from Mosaic law. Imagine how painful it must have been for all concerned to experience that splitting apart. They harshly judged one another, a practice common among various sects, according to Dead Sea writings. In fact, it appears there was hatred toward those with whom there was disagreement.

Is it any wonder the women were upset? Within only a few years of Jeshua's death, they were watching the tender shoots of religious revolution trampled as the men reverted right back to the old authoritarian model. That his teachings were not anchored is self-evident.

I asked James what role the women had after Jeshua was killed. He answered, "There was lots of caretaking by the women. However, I put up my shields. I'd get away so they couldn't go deeper." He explained that some of the women, particularly Mary Magdalene, tried to work with him and that he had let her get somewhat close. James did not offer anything that suggested his faction included women in any role other than as caretakers. And,

27. Edmund Wilson, *The Scrolls From The Dead Sea* (Oxford University Press, 1956), p. 27.

as this was reported by a strong, independent woman of today, I feel quite certain that, had it been different, she would have said so.

In order to better understand James and his relationship with Jeshua, I asked this client to move back in memory to when James was much younger, to a time when Jeshua was still living with the family. James recalled a joyful event, a Seder. The whole family was together, including the youngest boy, Juda. (Surprisingly little is said about this brother.) James explained that their father, Joseph, was very ill but perked up as the family sang because of his love of music. James described Jeshua as withdrawn, not participating in the singing. "He's being pulled. I can see it in his eyes and in his energy. He is pulled by a strong inner voice ... so strong he can almost not bear the surroundings. He needs time away."

James envied Jeshua's inner voice. He said, "All I hear is chatter. I can't still my mind. He does it so easily." I sympathized with James. What would it have been like to be Jeshua's younger brother? The entire community had awaited Jeshua's birth and recognized him as the Messiah, the Anointed One. Did James understand that? Not at the time. He felt envious, inferior, and sometimes downright angry that the responsibilities of the eldest son, Jeshua, fell instead on his, the second son's shoulders, and yet he enjoyed none of the status or privilege. As the eldest son, Jeshua inherited everything from Joseph—who, according to one client, was wealthy because of his carpentry business (which today would be the equivalent of an engineer's in terms of status and income). Because of Jeshua, James had no access to that wealth.

James' epiphany came at the instant of Jeshua's death. James made a deep connection with his brother by way of what we would today call an out-of-body experience. In discussing that part of her session, Karen said with great reverence, "I wish I could share what it was like to be out of my body and with him. It was profound. I never before understood how we are *eternal*. When he touched my hand and we were both out of our bodies, it felt much more real than in bodies. When Jeshua touched me, we went into *Oneness*."

Karen desired to heal the ancient wounds.

"I want to ask Jeshua to forgive me. He was the first-born, and the first-born has responsibilities. I felt as though I had the weight of the world on my shoulders. I resented his taking off and leaving things to me. Now I see that I didn't have to take on the weight of the world. I felt like Atlas. I was somewhat of a perfectionist. I accepted the job as figurehead and tried to lead to the best of my ability, but it felt like a bit of a curse."

I asked Karen what needed healing between James and his mother.

"There is no blame. I kept searching for her approval, trying to be like him ... that light! She held it out to me, 'Why can't you be more like your brother?' I'm now ready to let go of that. In truth, there is no need for forgiveness. I love her. I want her to be at peace as I am at peace."

Karen wrote to me three months after that session, saying, "I loved it that James learned nonjudgment. This is his wisdom. What has thrilled me is that I feel 'merged' with him. I do not feel the separation. [It is] as if I have assimilated his wisdom. In other words, I feel our Oneness—the Eternal Now—not separated by the veil of time and space."

I wrote back to Karen and thanked her for her letter, observing that her own healing through self-forgiveness and forgiving those who judged him/her, will help heal deep wounds from that time. Healing reaches across time, and it reaches across consciousness.

The oversoul which includes Karen and James spoke words of forgiveness. Through the process of regression, Karen helped herself by freeing her spirit of ancient envy, blame, resentment, and guilt. As James, she helped Myrium by forgiving her, thus also passing that forgiveness to present-day Hannah, who will perceive that forgiveness in some mystical way. The archetypes of James— *Reluctant Figurehead* and *Jealous Brother*—highly controlling and judgmental in his time, continue to evolve now through the gentle spirit of a modern woman.

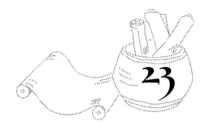

THE LAST DAYS OF THE SISTERHOOD

*M*yrium mourned, "I feel so sad for what my grandchildren have gone through. Their father was murdered. That is very hard on young children, and they deserve so much more. Mary has a lot to handle in taking care of them. She does get visitations from Jeshua. Well, the children do, too. Sometimes they can see him. Mary can always see him, which is what allows her to carry on. She gets strength from that, although she's strong anyway."

"What is her work as she sees it?"

"She devotes herself to the children and to him—as if he were still in a physical body. If the spirit moves her to do outreach, she does that."

"Does she have contact with the other apostles?"

"Cephas and Timothy come to see her. Bartholomew, too. James tries. It's such a struggle for him. He tries to be the peacemaker."

"Between whom?"

"Everybody. Nobody can control Paul, who is lit with the fire of certainty and righteousness. And God bless him for that, in that he's going different places [to spread the word]. Would that he could melt his stubbornness to let others in." Her head dropped, and she folded her hands in her lap. "Nobody comes to me."

Paul (through Nick) confirmed this in a regression session conducted after the publication of *The Messengers*. I had asked whether Mary had been consulted following Jeshua's death. He'd answered, "I don't recall her being consulted on any decisions that were made with the *apostuli*, the apostles, when they formed the Brotherhood. Nor was she consulted about their activities afterwards."[28]

"Where do you live out your last days?" Tradition has it that Myrium (Mother Mary) spent her last days in Ephesus with Timothy and John. I wondered what this client would report.

"I went to live in the North (which she later identified as somewhere in the Italian Alps). Timothy and Jonah take good care of me. Timothy is a good boy. He makes sure that I get what I need, that things are OK in the home. He [says he] feels blessed to be a part of the family. He's dutiful. There's a simple, precious beauty to his sense of duty. I can count on Timothy."

"Do you worry about Mary? Some apostles have been killed."

"We are laying low. The ones being killed are out there ... visible. Women aren't perceived as a threat. That's part of the protection. The men stole the thunder but also the visibility. They took the spotlight off Mary and the children. She's hardly given a thought at all."

"Do you see Mary Magdalene often?"

"She lives nearby. I can see her house from mine. We're in the mountains. Our cluster of houses are away from everything—the community and the politics. The community wouldn't be safe for us. When there was danger in Jerusalem, we slipped away, out of the eye of the storm. The problems are happening in the South. We are better off away."

"Where's Ruth?"

"She comes often to visit and lives with us sometimes, but her home is elsewhere. She comes to see me but is torn between here

---

28. G.W. Hardin, *The Days of Wonder: Dawn of a Great Tomorrow* (DreamSpeaker Creations, 2003), pp. 187-188.

and home [Rome]. Ruth's marriage to a Roman has helped us in some ways. Isn't it odd? They were the ones who killed him, and yet some also protect us."

"Please move forward to the last few months of your life." She took a deep breath and appeared as if she were in distress.

"I can't hold on. Oh, God. There's talk of moving back to be near Mount Carmel. I'm so tired, I don't want to move. They [the male apostles] all want us to come back. The men didn't forget us entirely. It's just that we weren't included. Before Jeshua was killed, we were part of the presentation—active. Now we women are more passive. It would be easier if we were closer."

"Please move forward to your death," I prompted Myrium.

"Where am I?[29] I know I'm dying. I'm starting to lift out of my body, but I feel myself struggling. I'm aware the body is dying before I can get out. I need to focus." She took a deep breath and brought her hands together. "I activate my energy and burst through [laughing] and then ... dance for joy, light and happy. I say goodbye to everyone. They are glad to know I've burst free. And then I go. I don't see the point in coming back in the ascended form as Jeshua did. I'm going on."

"Yes, keep going."

"I see Jeshua. [She cries] Son of Suns, bright as the sun. He fills my heart when I see him. I love him. He carries me into the light."

"What happens after the light?"

"I'm nearly mindless."

"Retain enough consciousness to describe your between-life state."

"Density of the formless ... lack of density of the formless. The expansion of the formless. Energy is swirling around me like a big soup. Random thought. Big expansion of energy." She could barely speak. Myrium was dead.

---

29. I didn't ask my client for clarification of where she died. However, Paul said, "[Mary] passed away in Ephesus. She had moved there after we had established a church community there. She was very close to Timothy. He watched over her the last couple of years." Ibid, p. 192.

Anarisa, Jeshua's first teacher, was also dead—killed when the entire Mount Carmel community was massacred. Sarah of Arimathea was safe for the time being in the British Isles. And what became of Mary Magdalene? There's a lot of excitement right now over the theory that Mary Magdalene was secreted out of Jerusalem for her safety and taken to the south of France to live. To date, I have no client material to lend credence to that theory (although northern Italy is close). There may be as many opinions about that as there are women tapping into the archetype, collective memories, or sacred records.

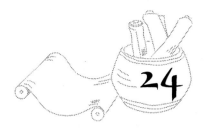

MYRIUM'S HEALING

T he desire on my clients' parts to heal old, deep wounds of shame and regret over the acts people committed in past lives; to get beyond the anger of being the target of other people's ignorance and cruelty; and finally to transcend the belief that the movement, which began two thousand years ago, had failed has been self-evident. Many women, perhaps most, who have tapped into these ancient memories reported they died angry or broken-hearted. Such strong feelings do carry over into the present. Is this why the Sisterhood is back today?

The following material comes from a get-together, a reunion of three prominent characters in this story: Myrium, Ruth and Cephas. To avoid confusion over who is talking, I will use their past-life names only. I had been working with these women separately but concurrently, and each had expressed an interest in meeting with other women with past-life memories of that time. I arranged for the four of us to spend several hours together. After a few minutes of getting acquainted, the women began talking as if they recognized each other. I had thought I might do a group regression to help them, but it wasn't necessary. I just sat back and turned on the tape recorder. The following took place near the end of the meeting.

"I felt so alienated after Jeshua died," said Ruth. "I didn't have any contact with you [Mother]; something weird happened. I felt, not alone, but that you weren't there."

Myrium sighed. "I may have been there physically but not there emotionally."

"Yes, I had never seen you like that," Ruth said. "You would sit and not talk. It wasn't like you. You used to talk a lot. You were very outspoken. But all of a sudden, you wouldn't talk. It was like you were in an altered state. I remember hollering at you, I just kept hollering, 'Mother!'"

Ruth continued. "When you were in that state I thought you went with him—spiritually. Wherever he went, you went with him, and what was left was ... " Myrium nodded agreement. "You get it, don't you?" asked Ruth. She believed that because of Myrium's grief at her son's death and the frustration of not being listened to by the men, her spirit had left to be with Jeshua.

Myrium said that the problem now was her identifying with the part that was emptied out, not the part that went with Jeshua. In other words, in present time, she was carrying the grief, frustration, and emptiness that she believed were a part of her experience two thousand years ago.

Because these women were not only healers in the present but were remembering how to work with healing energy from the past, I asked if they would be willing to work with Myrium now. We recognized that we had the exceptional power of a triad with which to work. All readily agreed. Myrium was in great anguish and afraid that she couldn't do it, but with Cephas' gentle encouragement, she sank into the chair and closed her eyes. Cephas took the lead, placing her hands on Myrium's lower back. She directed Ruth to touch her feet and me to place my hands on Myrium's head.

Myrium began to sob.

Cephas asked, "What was your greatest fear in that lifetime?"

"To lose him," was the choking reply.

"You have identified with your fear. Now you need to identify with your faith. Your faith of who he was and who you were."

Myrium cried, "How do I identify with my faith? I have ... I have forgotten. To go through life being prepared for his conception, then seeing him born and how beautiful he was ... knowing I was holding the Promise in my hands ... to nurture that and raise him and give everything I could in order to cultivate it ... just so he could ... " She broke down again. "What happened to him ... it seems too cruel!" She wept bitterly.

"May I say something?" asked Cephas. Myrium nodded. "I feel that you are also speaking metaphorically of something inside you that was conceived. That was your faith, your ever-strong faith which you nurtured and developed. Your baby boy was there, but at the same time, you were nurturing *your* faith. But then, when he was crucified, a very human part of you cut it right off."

Myrium countered, "But of course. I was crushed."

"While another part of you went on and proceeded with the work. You split right down the middle. So you need to integrate back into the fullness of who you are, being willing to trust yourself enough now to fully connect with your higher self."

"But how do I heal the split?" Myrium asked. I suggested she tune into that part that went with Jeshua because she knew the grieving, empty, and angry part very well.

Myrium became very quiet. She began breathing deeply and then reported, "I have a feeling of flying through time and space. There is this feeling of being almost one with him, but not. I'm soothed and comforted. Here, I am beyond the mundane stuff of the world; here, I escape from it. The question is, why wouldn't I want to be here? I feel like I just attached to him; wherever he went, I went. It is like a baby that attaches to a parent. I just want to merge with him. I don't want to go back to that body." She began to cry. "I feel him shoving me away, making me go back." Her sobs turned to wailing. "He says I can't go with him. I feel so alone. I am abandoned. I wanted to be with him, and Jeshua pushed me away."

Suddenly Ruth called out, "Mother, I need you. I need you so much. Please come back. I'm so sorry you feel so alone. You are not alone. Please know we love you."

Myrium appeared bitter. "I can't hear you. Without him, I am nothing." A few moments passed, and she shook her head, sadly. "I know that isn't true."

"We all felt that way, though," agreed Cephas. "We all felt that way. He embodied it so much better than we could even dream of, and we really clung to that, so we clung to him."

Myrium sniffed and rubbed the tears from her eyes and cheeks. "God. It is so 'off' from what the teachings were. I feel so wrong to cling to him. It is so wrong, because the teachings tell us that it is all in here." She pointed to her heart.

Cephas nodded. "Yes, we had a very difficult time embodying everything ourselves. But, Myrium, we did. Eventually, we did ... as best we could. It wasn't like him, but it was the best we could do."

I asked this woman if she felt able to work with her Myrium self to forgive all the things she was judging about herself. "You know how to do this. Myrium participated in the healings. She knows how to forgive herself." I prompted, "'I forgive myself for ... '"

"For thinking I'm wrong for attaching to him. I forgive myself for attaching to him. I forgive myself for not fully embodying the Christ state as he did, and I forgive myself for wanting to leave. I don't trust this. Oh, God. I forgive myself for not trusting God. I forgive myself for not trusting Jeshua. And I forgive myself for not trusting myself. I forgive myself for letting my vision be obscured and for blaming myself for that."

Cephas gently added, "And for blaming others. You did a lot of that."

"And for blaming others. I'm sorry." She was now laughing and crying. "I forgive myself for not fully understanding everything. I forgive myself for feelings of not being a good enough mother to all my children. And I forgive myself for thinking that it was my fault the Church was founded in the way it was."

I urged, "Please let that one land, solidly."

"I forgive myself for taking so long to forgive myself."

I asked her if there were any other people she wanted to forgive. She felt that she needed to forgive Mary Magdalene. "I think she got angry with me when I withdrew. She tried to console me and be with me, and I think she got very frustrated with me." She sighed. "I need to forgive Paul."

Cephas laughed. "We're all working on that one."

"He was operating as best he could, just like all of us" said Myrium.

Cephas again coached, "So, that is what you are opening up— the memory of your faith."

Several minutes passed as we three continued to hold the energy in place. Myrium continued to cry softly. Finally, I asked her if she needed anything. She said she needed her sight to be opened.

Cephas asked me to open my hands in a cup form above Myrium's head. I felt an enormous jolt of energy and a rushing of air. It lasted for several minutes.

Myrium said, "I feel this intense energy rushing in, down-loading from above, popping things open, especially in my head— the pineal gland. I feel this flood of energy and things popping open. Yes, my eyes are open. My spiritual eyes." She looked at each of us. "Thank you all for your help."

Ruth's eyes were full of tears. "You had such courage, wisdom and integrity. I wanted to be a part of that, too. I wanted to be that also. That is why it was such a shock when you weren't there. But I realized how much fear there was for me in losing you, and how I need to forgive you. In the middle of your work, I finally understood what it must have been like for you. I think we are all caught up in our own story. Whatever healing came about this afternoon, it is important for Ruth, too."

"It is so powerful, isn't it? I can really feel it, too," said Cephas. "I worried for a long time because I felt your lack of trust."

Myrium smiled back at her. "You know, what I feel now is that you were trying very hard to keep a foot here and stay connected there, and it was really, really hard. I commend you for it."

Tears sprung to Cephas' eyes. "I can't tell you how much that means to me. I feel this deep love for you, and as you were going through your process, I came to understand that I had deep integrity and didn't betray you."

Ruth ended this beautiful reunion with an observation. "This has opened up a whole new world for me that is more concrete. What we have done is bring this from another plane into more consciousness. We have brought something very useful into the world."

These women moved past anger and despair and into action. They reclaimed their faith and trust. They remembered to love each other. "We didn't fail two thousand years ago, and we cannot fail today."

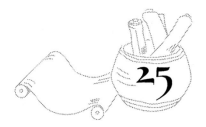

The Sisterhood
Today and Tomorrow

*I*t has not been my intention, in writing *The Lost Sisterhood*—nor do I think it is the intention of any of the people whose stories are within these pages—to try to convince you that they *were* these historical figures in their past lives. While they may well have been, that is a personal decision they will make for themselves, and your belief is a personal decision for you. My intention has been to bring into awareness how it contributes to the evolutionary process to tap into these stories, these archetypes, and to look at an ancient culture through modern eyes.

The cover story of the December 22, 2003, issue of *U.S. News and World Report* was "The Jesus Code: America Is Rethinking the Messiah—*Again*." Journalists Linda Kulman and Jay Tolson wrote how, beginning with Thomas Jefferson, Americans have "tinkered with the traditional image of Jesus ... [to] suit their present needs." They quoted Stephen Prothero, chairman of the religion department at Boston University and author of a new book, *American Jesus: How the Son of God Became a National Icon* (Farrar Straus & Giroux, 2003), as saying, "What Americans have seen in

[Jesus], has been an expression of their own hopes and fears—a reflection not simply of some 'wholly other' divinity but also of themselves." The article also addressed the huge success of Dan Brown's novel *The Da Vinci Code*, by quoting Richard Wightman Fox, author of *Jesus in America* (HarperSanFrancisco, 2004), who said Brown spoke to the desire for a very human, approachable savior and a contemporary yearning "for a female sacred presence."

This is an apt description of what I see is happening. The journalists' curious choice of the word "tinkered," however, trivializes this groundswell of people who are reimagining Christianity—*again*. It is hardly "tinkering" to participate in an evolution of consciousness. Over the millennia we have had periods of extreme darkness. One of my clients referred to those times—like the era when women healers and seers were condemned to death in the name of God—as ages of "endarkenment." We've also enjoyed periods of great leaps forward. Jesus/Jeshua and his close friends and family were a soul cluster, born together to usher in one of those periods of enlightenment when they spoke of God not as a jealous and judging God, but as a loving Mother/Father God. They planted seeds of evolution. I am convinced that in the divine order of things, it was not imagined that the world would change in the few short years that he was teaching. Society has had two thousand years of living with the ideas that he and his extended family brought to us. Some of our experimentation with Christianity has been the antithesis of what he taught. Some has been very close to what he was teaching.

People who report resonance to that time have incarnated at *this* time to participate in the next leap forward. All appear to share several significant beliefs: The teachings of Jeshua became distorted; the power of the image of the crucified Christ was usurped in the name of controlling people; the movement was thrown out of balance when the men stopped listening to the women; and the followers "weren't good enough" to continue his work after his crucifixion. Therefore, most of them internalized deep feelings of guilt, shame, anger, and failure. The other belief that they all have in common is that they are back now with another chance to to make things even better.

Some people make light of so-called New Age thinking, calling it idealistic, wishful, naive, simplistic, etc. Some even say it is a dangerous indulgence to believe in an ideal world, or heaven on earth. They are worried that, in being idealistic, we will forget to admit to the failings in people (our shadow aspects) and therefore be vulnerable to a fall of our civilization—just as Rome fell, just as many civilizations have fallen. However, the fact that we long for an ideal world means that innately we know that it is possible. I hold that vision. But, if we destroy this world, our beautiful planet, we will have lost that opportunity. Many scientists have warned us that at the present rate of population growth, the pollution in our air and water, global warming, and the misuse of technology, humankind has only a fifty-fifty chance of surviving the twenty-first century. Add to this the warmongering, corporate greed, and increasing violence, and the chance for survival decreases even more.

I have worked diligently for the past eighteen years or so, calling forth numerous past lives of my own in order to heal from trauma and distorted thinking, or to make amends for the suffering I have caused others. Two thousand years ago, I was He Who Watches Over Spirit, a quiet, unassuming monk. I never left the monastery, but instead waited as students came to me. Today, I am neither unassuming nor patient. We don't have time for anyone of good will to be passive. The Sisterhood is back—back with a motivating dissatisfaction with the way things are and with the energy, vision, and spirit to make changes. As a member of that Sisterhood, I'm doing what I can to empower women to be their own spiritual authority *and* to end five thousand years of valuing masculine principles over feminine ones. Jeshua taught: "When you make male and female into a single one, ... then you will enter the kingdom." I take great pleasure in working with women and men who strive to achieve this balance, this *Sacred Marriage* within themselves.

Throughout history, it has only required a small percentage of the population, whose consciousness had expanded, to move the entire body ahead. We call that *conscious evolution*. It is essential we take that next leap forward—now! I call on the Sisterhood to come forth and make noise. I call on the men to listen to the women! I call on all of you women who are able to tap into the archetype of Mary Magdalene, and other visionary women, to be bold and assume your rightful place as leaders.

Printed in the United States
40640LVS00004B/13-24